Updating
CLASSIC AMERICA
COLONIALS

Design Ideas for Renovating, Remodeling, and Building New

Matthew Schoenherr

The Taunton Press

The Taunton Press
Inspiration for hands-on living®

The Taunton Press, Inc., 63 South Main Street, PO Box 5506, Newtown, CT 06470-5506
e-mail: tp@taunton.com

Distributed by Publishers Group West

EDITORS: Roger Yepsen, Peter Chapman

DESIGN AND LAYOUT: Lori Wendin

ILLUSTRATOR: Christine Erikson

PHOTOGRAPHER: Grey Crawford

COVER PHOTOGRAPHERS: Grey Crawford, Woodruff/Brown Photography

Updating Classic America: Colonials was originally published in hardcover
in 2003 by The Taunton Press, Inc.

LIBRARY OF CONGRESS CATALOGING-IN-PUBLICATION DATA
Schoenherr, Matthew.
  Colonials : design ideas for renovating, remodeling, and building new /
Matthew Schoenherr.
        p. cm. — (Updating classic America)
Includes index.
    ISBN-13 978-156158-564-9 hardcover
    ISBN-10 1-56158-564-5 hardcover
    ISBN-10 1-56158-743-5 paperback w/flaps
    ISBN-13 978-156158-743-8 paperback w/flaps
1. Architecture, Domestic—United States—Designs and plans. 2.
Architecture, Colonial—United States—Influence. I. Title: Design
ideas for renovating, remodeling, and building new. II. Title. III.
Series.
  NA7208 .S36 2003
    728'.37—dc21

The following brand names/manufacturers are trademarks: Monopoly®, Volvo®, Dumpster®,
Technicolor®, Hardie Board™

Printed in Singapore
10 9 8 7 6 5 4 3 2 1

For Nikolaus and Helene,
who came to hatch their own
little colony in 1953.

Acknowledgments

DON'T BE FOOLED BY THE SINGLE NAME that appears on the front cover—many
individuals helped to put this project together, and they deserve a warm thank you:

The only expression I've seen on Peter Chapman's face is a wide smile. He is a
supportive, caring editor and has given me my first chance at writing about architecture at a time rather unexpected in my career as a practicing architect. Thanks
Peter. And thanks to series editor Roger Yepsen who has taken the draft of the
manuscript and boiled it down to a smooth elixir. Thanks also go to the energetic
Paula Schlosser, Wendi Mijal, and Robyn Aitken. Photographer Grey Crawford is a
blast to hang out with, and he fueled my enthusiasm immeasurably as packet after
packet of fresh film arrived at my office during the summer. Of course, the architects and Colonial homeowners whose projects and homes appear in this book were
so very kind to unroll the drawings and open the doors to these wonderful houses.

I've discovered that I have to write with the headphones on and the music
cranked to an absurd level of volume, so thanks to Natalie Merchant, k.d. lang,
Delerium, Blue Six, Shelby Lynne, Pink Floyd, Dan Hicks and the Hot Licks, Joni
Mitchell, and Diana Krall!

Big thanks to my partner in professional practice, Kevin Huelster, who tirelessly
watched the fort during my partial hiatus, and to *Capes* author Jane Gitlin for her
ideas and patient ear.

I've saved the best for last; thank you Beth for your support, patience, and love—
and thanks also to those three little people that follow us around wherever we go.

CONTENTS

INTRODUCTION

IN MY CONNECTICUT ARCHITECTURAL PRACTICE, we have several Colonial renovations underway at any given point—homes that are being enlarged, updated, modernized, altered, or restored. Of the houses that come through our office door and wind up on our 21-in. computer monitors, Colonials are the most common.

The owners' requests are similar—to improve or enlarge the house to fit their lifestyles and their needs. Sometimes we're even asked to help make a house look a little more authentic, if it hasn't been around for a century or two. And I oblige them happily. This house type has a past that no others can match, with such offshoots as Georgian, Dutch Colonial, and the Adams style. Even simple farmhouses have their roots in the

Colonial gene pool. And about a hundred years ago, just when the style seemed to have been exhausted from being used over and over, a new variation was hatched—the Colonial Revival!

My appreciation for Colonials may have come from a vicarious experience through my wife. She grew up in a Connecticut Saltbox originally constructed in 1789. There was a historic magic to the house. You could sense something there that I can only describe as an American Spirit. Maybe it was her parents' wonderful collection of American antiques and folk art. Perhaps it was any one of the three fireplaces that you could practically walk into. But this isn't to say that a house has to be ancient to conjure up this feeling. I can visit a Colonial built within the past several years and that same spirit is apt to come across if the home has been carefully proportioned and detailed. Colonials can feel like more than a house. They can feel like a place.

This book has been written to show real-life renovations that can preserve or reinforce the style. Some of the houses you'll see are very small in scale, with projects you might easily and inexpensively undertake on your own. Other projects are far more ambitious and will likely require the professional services of an architect and a general contractor. There are many avenues you can take to express your own vision for a Colonial home. Read on—and participate in the Updating of Classic America.

CHAPTER ONE

THE AMERICAN COLONIAL HOME

This renovated Newport, Rhode Island, neighborhood stands as a tribute to the Colonial house type. Recognized as American classics, Colonial houses are enjoying a resurgence of interest.

L ET'S BEGIN BY CHALLENGING our imaginations. Get comfortable and picture a home—a Colonial home. Maybe it's the house where you lived as a child, or your grandparents' home. Maybe it's where you're sitting right now. Concentrate on what you see—the form of the house, the composition of the facade, the spot where the chimney leaves the roof, the depth of the eaves, and the types of materials. Now envision the interior. What's inside? How are the rooms laid out? Where is the stair, the fireplace? Feel the walls, see the finishes, look at the windows, the doors, the details...

AMERICA'S FIRST AND LASTING STYLE

This challenge was a kind of test—a test where there are only right answers, because the possibilities are as unlimited as your memory and dreams will allow. The homey image of the Colonial is often depicted in novels, television shows, and feature films. Colonial homes have

Colonial homes have developed a reputation as blandly designed development homes for a homogeneous population, but the style doesn't have to be tame. This updated classic has been personalized with a dynamic interior treatment that conveys one of many possibilities for the type.

gable roof ⁀ A roof with a single sloping plane on either side of a central ridge.

even been offered as the grand prize in sweepstakes contests.

Real-life Colonials come in many styles: the Early American Saltbox, Dutch Colonial, French Colonial, and Colonial Revival are just a few examples. You may not know all of the names, but chances are you've seen them in many places—as the compelling centerpieces of gated estates, or lined up along the streets of established neighborhoods. Colonial homes constructed 300 years ago border many a picturesque New England green, while recently constructed Colonials stand watch over suburban home sites across America and offer their owners state-of-the-art amenities.

The Colonial's two-story **gable roof** form casts a satisfying silhouette. It's not quite the Monopoly® house—author and architect Jane Gitlin confirms that those little green houses are the Cape Cod style—but more like the hotel (the big red ones). Older than our nation, the Colonial is the quintessential American family home. It has come to stand as a symbol of traditional values and a promise of a stable, nurturing lifestyle. That's because it's a home with roots.

Charming as the images seem, there can be problems with such a home. The floor plan may be poorly laid out, the kitchen and bathrooms may be in need of remodeling, or there could be too few bedrooms and not enough storage space to accommodate a growing family. In this book, we'll take a look at several of the styles that make up this popular American house type and examine how architects, designers, and homeowners have altered these superlative houses to make them better places for a family to live and grow. We'll include strategies for creating additions that work well and ideas for new Colonial homes. But first, let's examine the parts and pieces that define the basic Colonial house type.

HALLMARKS OF COLONIAL DESIGN

The historic timeline of the Colonial home begins with the nation's first settlers from Europe and continues to the present day. Amazingly, the architectural elements that define the Colonial have been with us more than three centuries, a telling sign that there is so much about this straightforward design that just *works*.

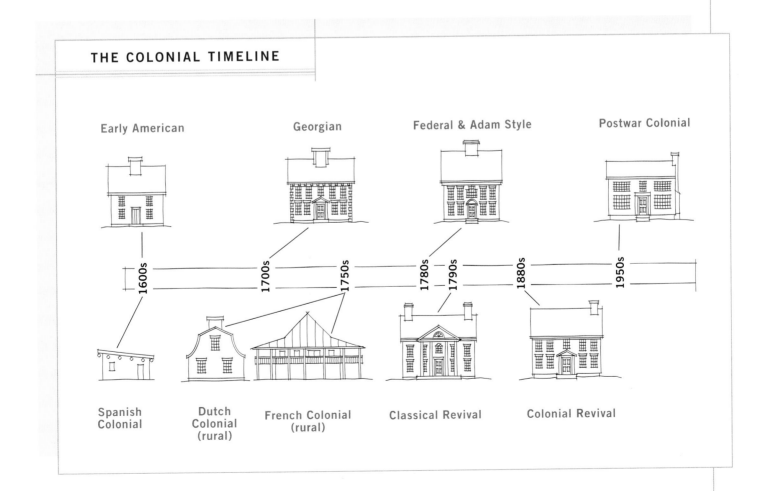

THE COLONIAL TIMELINE

Early American — Georgian — Federal & Adam Style — Postwar Colonial

1600s — 1700s — 1750s — 1780s — 1790s — 1880s — 1950s

Spanish Colonial — Dutch Colonial (rural) — French Colonial (rural) — Classical Revival — Colonial Revival

Early American Houses

MUCH OF WHAT WE SEE in early Colonial houses was brought to the New World from Europe. Colonists used the building techniques they were familiar with back home. In the northern colonies, a large stone chimney sat in the center of a rectangular plan. The chimney contained two fireboxes, one for each of the lower floor's two rooms. A third firebox was sometimes located at the back of the house, where summer cooking could take place outside. Later, these outside areas were built over, then entirely enclosed, creating the popular Saltbox (also known as a Catslide in the South). Southern colonists enjoyed a milder climate, and fireplaces were positioned at the ends of the house. This cleared the way for a central hallway with doors at front and back for cross ventilation.

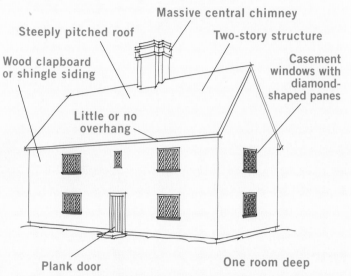

Massive central chimney

Steeply pitched roof

Two-story structure

Wood clapboard or shingle siding

Casement windows with diamond-shaped panes

Little or no overhang

Plank door

One room deep

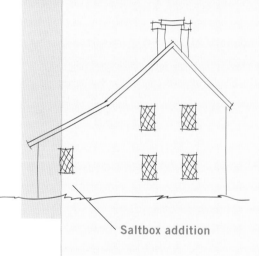

Saltbox addition

Early Colonial rooms were small and dark. Ceiling heights were just over 6 ft. in many cases, and window openings were few and less than generous. These rooms could be heated more efficiently by the massive stone fireplace, which was kept burning throughout the day and radiated heat to the sleeping chambers on the upper floor at night. Windows originally were casements with diamond-shaped panes called *quarries,* but virtually all surviving homes of this long-past era have been retrofitted with hung-sash windows.

Take a fresh look at a Colonial house, and you'll see the strategies that have influenced American housing design again and again. Although the basic floor plan and the simple structure may seem unremarkable, understanding these fundamental patterns is an important step toward achieving success in your own addition or renovation. Frank Lloyd Wright said, "A physician can bury his mistakes, but an architect can only advise his clients to plant ivy"—a wry reminder that the per-

manence of buildings makes it all the more important that we take extra care in their design.

The form

The primary shape of a Colonial is a two-story rectangular box with a sloped roof. Living spaces are on the first floor, with bedrooms positioned above. The roof ridge commonly runs parallel with the front facade—that is, the long side of the rectangle. You'll find that a gable roof tops off most Colonial houses, but **gambrel**

ABOVE, **The style evokes** a stable image of home, and many homeowners aspire to it. A Colonial is usually a step up from a Cape or Bungalow in size— the type of home where a family can really stretch out and grow.

LEFT, **Colonials lend themselves** well to the creation of historic reproductions or to the use of architectural metaphors that create a fresh sense of the style without being too literal.

The rigor of the Colonial form is seen as too formal by some, but other families find a comforting simplicity in the wholesome shape, and elegance in the stoic imagery.

gambrel roof ⌐ A modified gable roof with two pitches on either side of the ridge.

hip roof ⌐ A roof sloped on all sides, similar to a pyramid.

cross-gable ⌐ A gable roof that intersects or projects perpendicular to the main roof.

portico ⌐ A covered porch, supported by posts or columns and typically surrounding the entryway to the home.

and **hip roofs** also were used. The roof may have a **cross-gable** forming a **portico** over the front entry. The type of roof can indicate the origin of a very old Colonial house—for example, Colonials from the region occupied by Dutch settlers had gambrel roofs—but this is less true of newer homes in which creative liberties were often taken.

Additions to the main form may serve any number of functions. A couple of hundred years ago, these appendages were used as butteries, kitchens, and even slaves' quarters or for livestock. Today, additions are more likely to contain a garage with a connecting laundry and a mudroom, or a family room with a bedroom or two above. In just about any historic period, you'll find that these additions are out the back or to the sides of the main structure—rarely in front. Furthermore, additions to the sides typically step back and down a little, placing emphasis on the main house and its carefully arranged front facade. Both homeowners of the past and today's architects have adopted an architectural concept called *hierarchy*: A building exterior expresses its organization better if you can read into it an orderly progression of forms. The old children's rhyme, "Big house, little house, back house, barn," comes to mind. The image is that of a large central house with diminishing additions popping out of the sides and back. There is a comforting logic to the arrangement—and as a practical point, first-time visitors won't have to hunt to find the front door, centered in the main structure.

A portico addition can be relatively small in size and still be thoroughly useful to shelter a group of friends arriving for dinner during a downpour. The compact design of this portico doesn't interfere with the existing windows to either side or above.

COLONIAL ROOF VARIATIONS

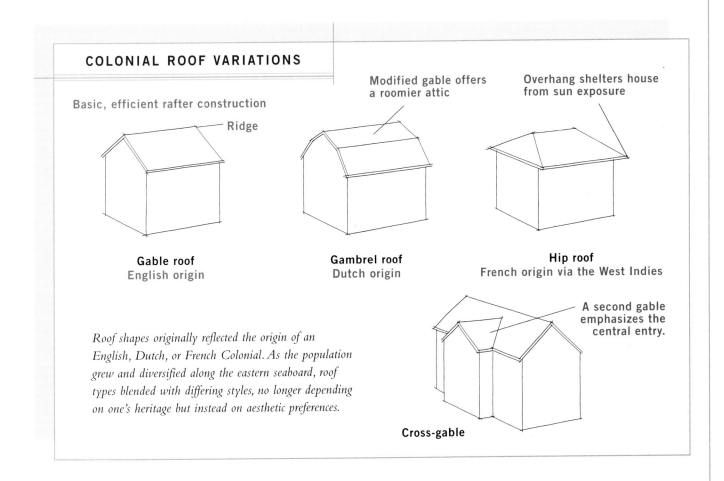

Basic, efficient rafter construction

Ridge

Gable roof
English origin

Modified gable offers a roomier attic

Gambrel roof
Dutch origin

Overhang shelters house from sun exposure

Hip roof
French origin via the West Indies

A second gable emphasizes the central entry.

Cross-gable

Roof shapes originally reflected the origin of an English, Dutch, or French Colonial. As the population grew and diversified along the eastern seaboard, roof types blended with differing styles, no longer depending on one's heritage but instead on aesthetic preferences.

Colonials usually have an explicitly formal appearance to the front, but an informal atmosphere can be created on the opposite side. Ordinarily, the rear of the home presents fewer limitations and greater opportunities when adding on.

The facade

While other styles have forms and features that can be juggled extensively and still retain a family resemblance, this isn't true of the Colonial. From one to the next, Colonials retain a rigorously consistent two-story form and an unerring approach in the composition of the front facade. Colonial facades are marked with the strict spacing of windows—three, five, and sometimes seven across on the second floor—above a central front door. These key attributes were defined long ago, back when the medieval houses of the first colonists began to evolve beyond mere shelter.

If you walk around a traditional Colonial, you'll notice that the concern for specific window placement relaxes toward the back. A departure from the style's rigor could be justified on this informal, private side of the house. As is true today, the rear facade was often

Centuries ago, the dining room was referred to as the "best room," a place where a guest would be presented with gracious hospitality among the family's finest possessions. For many, the dining room remains an important setting for family gatherings and long-standing traditions.

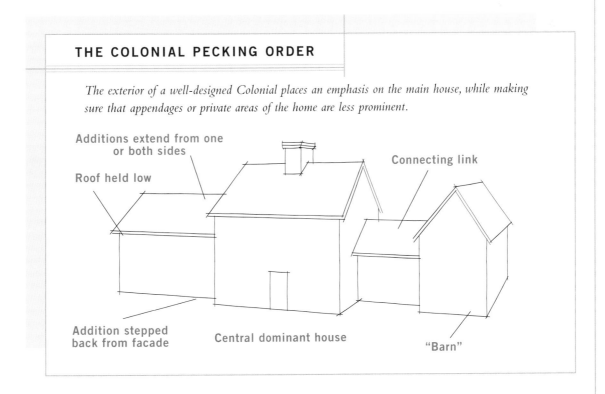

THE COLONIAL PECKING ORDER

The exterior of a well-designed Colonial places an emphasis on the main house, while making sure that appendages or private areas of the home are less prominent.

Additions extend from one or both sides

Roof held low

Connecting link

Addition stepped back from facade

Central dominant house

"Barn"

Northern and Southern Colonials

VARIATIONS

☆ **BECAUSE OF DIFFERENCES IN CLIMATE,** two fundamental patterns of constructing Colonials developed along the eastern seaboard. In the northern colonies, heating was more of a concern than cooling, and houses generally were built with a massive central chimney that would spread heat evenly through the rooms.

Good ventilation for cooling was a requirement in the South, and an open central hall allowed a flow of air between front and back. The chimneys were at the ends of the house so that the unwanted heat from cooking would radiate away to the exterior.

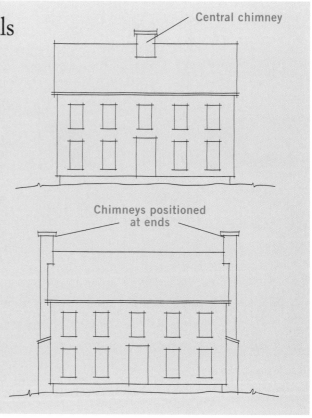

Central chimney

Chimneys positioned at ends

more expressive in nature, with windows placed so that they let in light where it was most desired. Or, room shapes bulged outward as dictated by the need for interior space. Over time, the rear facade is apt to acquire an ungainly collection of projections and additions, and the trained eye of an architect may be needed to sort things out.

The plan

You've probably heard the term *center hall Colonial,* referring to a layout with a central front door and a corresponding entry hall within. In Colonials of the northern states, the staircase is positioned behind this door with the *public* rooms to either side—a formal living room to one side and a study or a dining room to the

A familiar floor plan: The center hall accommodates the staircase to the second floor, while formal rooms flank either side. Undeniably functional, this elegant stair is also the stage for a dramatic appearance from the bedrooms above.

Dutch and French Colonials

WHILE THE ENGLISH COLONIZED the lion's share of the eastern seaboard, the Dutch occupied the general region of New York's Hudson Valley. Their houses often featured a multi-sloped gambrel roof with a gently flaring eaves instead of the steep gable common to the English houses. The Dutch Colonial generally appeared as a one-story structure with a fully habitable attic under the handsome, roomy gambrel roof. Dormers were built into the roof for light and ventilation.

Unlike English and Dutch houses, the early French Colonials didn't have an obvious model in their home-

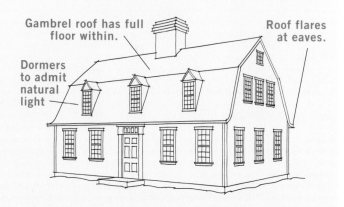

Gambrel roof has full floor within.

Roof flares at eaves.

Dormers to admit natural light

land. The design inspiration may have come from French settlements in the West Indies, where cooling was more of a concern than heating. The homes were built on stilts that extended upward to a hip roof. This pavilion-like roof extended well beyond the exterior walls of the house to create a protective veranda, shading the home. For ventilation, nearly every room had tall openings with swinging windows or doors leading to the covered area outside. The ceilings were high, unlike their northern counterparts, allowing for operable transoms across the tops of both doors and windows to further improve ventilation.

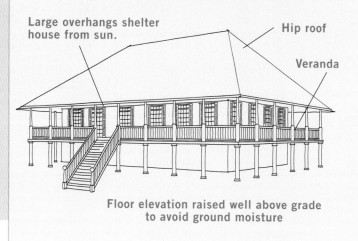

Large overhangs shelter house from sun.

Hip roof

Veranda

Floor elevation raised well above grade to avoid ground moisture

other. In the South, the plan is largely the same, except that a central hall runs entirely through the house to a back door, which can be opened to increase ventilation in the humid climate. In both northern and southern examples, the informal *private* kitchen and family spaces are at the rear of the house.

The use of two stories allows double the living area to be constructed on a relatively compact foundation, while quite neatly dividing living spaces below and

sleeping spaces above. At the top of the stair, a hallway connects the bedrooms. Master bedrooms as we know them today became common in suburban homes after World War II and often are positioned over the living room. Stacking the two big spaces, one over the other, allows for some structural economies.

In a Colonial, the rooms are *rooms*. That is, they are strongly defined by walls. You'll find no open-planning concepts in an older Colonial; the interior views through the home are limited entirely by what you can glimpse down a hall or through a doorway.

GOING BEYOND COLONIAL BASICS

Set foot in a typical Colonial home, and you'll quickly recognize how poorly utilized the floor area tends to be. There is more space devoted to formal rooms than most of us need in a home today, leaving too little for the rooms where a family really wants to flop down and stretch out. Family spaces often need to be enlarged, added on entirely, or converted from existing rooms.

Because the Colonial has a second floor, there is little opportunity for varying the ceiling height in the lower rooms. The result is a sameness from room to room and even from house to house, giving the Colonial a reputation among architects as being less than inspiring when it's time to renovate. It takes a good helping of creativity and even a dash of courage to break loose from the basic box.

ABOVE, **A change in ceiling** heights can bring a welcome variety in the experience of space, but the first floor of a Colonial, with another floor overhead, doesn't lend itself to raised ceilings with tall expanses of glass. This spacious family room is created within a less confining one-story addition.

LEFT, **The rooms in older** Colonials were designed to contain very specific activities. Today, we have less of a need to close rooms off from one another and generally desire more versatility and better communication between spaces.

THE CAPTAIN BILLINGS HOUSE

Tavernkeeper's
quarters

Tavern

Before

Rear extension

Dining room

Terrace

Laundry

Box window
admits extra light.

Kitchen

New
French
doors

Jack's study

Pantry

Break-
fast

Living
room

Den

Door replaced
with window

Entry hall

Melodee's
study

After

But when the familiar rooms are rethought, the result can be quite amazing, as the expected and average are transformed into the surprising and unique. The house we'll look at next is an example of how one home has emerged from such a remarkable transformation. Once a small tavern that had fallen to severe neglect, the Dutch Colonial is now a revived residence that contains the kind of spatial variety that goes beyond Colonial basics.

A CLASSIC COLONIAL RECONSTRUCTION

Richard "Skip" Broom, a Connecticut contractor and developer, is so devoted to Early American Colonial homes that he rescues condemned structures destined for demolition or fire department training exercises. He and his crew catalog, dismantle, move, and reconstruct houses deteriorated to the point that they've become a blight to the neighborhood.

Many of us wouldn't look twice at these tumble-down hulks with sapling trees sprouting between the rafters—there just doesn't seem to be anything worth salvaging. But Skip views them with an unusual degree of optimism, and he has moved several Colonials to a rural Connecticut development named Sterling City.

Reinterpreting an original

Jack and Melodee's long, low Dutch Colonial was built in 1753 in Salem, Connecticut. It is divided into discrete, low-ceilinged rooms connected by narrow doorways. What's most unusual are the two chimneys. They're not grouped together in the center of the house, as was typical for a northern Colonial, or positioned at the exterior walls, as would have been done in the South. The reason for this is the structure's history—it once

ABOVE, **Dutch Colonials make** use of a roomy gambrel roof for the second-floor bedrooms. Dormers admit natural light and fresh air to each bedroom. Back in the 1700s, this home was a tavern that hosted road-weary travelers.

LEFT, **With little to go on,** the developer had to reconstruct this old home in his imagination after his crew painstakingly cataloged and dismantled the structure.

You'd expect to see only windows in an end wall well above ground level, but here a protective rail has been installed to allow the use of French doors—the near equivalent of a balcony. This addition takes advantage of the sloped site, providing room on the basement level to enjoy natural light and access to the rear yard.

served as a tavern for local folks and travelers. One chimney warmed the tavern's customers, while the other warmed the owner's sleeping area.

In adapting the Billings Tavern, Skip followed traditional practice and added on only at the rear, keeping the new addition mostly out of sight from the unpaved streets of Sterling City. The front and side facades have been left intact, retaining the traditional Colonial composition of uniformly spaced windows about the door and the Dutch Colonial's row of dormers in the gambrel roof. Skip replaced the door that led to the tavern keeper's private quarters with a window; as he points out, the house is an *adaptive reconstruction*, not a restoration.

The addition provides space for a modern kitchen, albeit with a traditional look, and a modestly sized

ABOVE, **The preferred way** to add onto a Colonial is to place the addition to the side or to the rear. The new extension to the right contains a kitchen, pantry, and dining room.

BELOW, **This is one of several** masonry fireplaces that were carefully dismantled and then reassembled after the home was moved.

This kitchen creates a transition between the old house and the new addition. The ceiling remains low, as in the original structure, and is enlivened with reclaimed chestnut beams. The new dining room beyond has a high ceiling and lots of light, welcome features in a room where the owners enjoy entertaining.

informal dining room. These spaces are open in plan, allowing Jack and Melodee to stretch out and relax with friends—perhaps the way travelers once did in the old tavern. The single-story addition allows a high, sloped ceiling in the dining room, with tall windows transmitting light through to the kitchen. Having a space with high headroom is a welcome variation from the low ceilings found throughout the original home.

A kitchen transition

Jack and Melodee's new kitchen makes the transition between the original house and the new dining room. Skip chose to keep a low ceiling over the kitchen, and

he introduced reclaimed hand-hewn beams overhead for their hearty Early American character—an appropriate backdrop for the owners' collection of antique furniture and decorative objects.

A pantry fitted with plenty of useful storage is located adjacent to the kitchen. A separate pantry area lessens the burden on kitchen storage, meaning the kitchen can be smaller and have fewer cabinets. Jack and Melodee's kitchen and pantry are carefully sized to suit the small-scale character of the home. And because pantry shelves and cabinets don't have to be as high in quality as those in the kitchen, they can be left to appear rustic or utilitarian at a substantial savings.

The living room is thought to have been the tavern's main room. The front facade appears much as it once did, but to the rear of the living room, tradition was relaxed somewhat and French doors have been installed to offer pastoral views and give access to a new blue-stone terrace.

The pine trim and cabinetry surrounding the living room fireplace is original to the house, as is the opposite paneled wall. This rich millwork had been hidden behind wallpaper for more than a century. On either side of the fireplace, doors lead to a pair of small home offices for Melodee and Jack, where they can tend to their professional lives—and, when needed, the nearby fire.

Stair ways and means

The original staircase couldn't be reused because it was too narrow to comply with modern building codes and would have been downright dangerous in the event of a fire. Skip constructed a new stair and chose a square-edge vertical **baluster** to support the stout handrail. He also added scroll onlays at the **stringer,** based on a design from a pattern book popular about the time of the Revolutionary War. When Jack and Melodee retire to their bedroom each night, their slippered feet are still in touch with the old tavern—the staircase is new, but the chestnut **treads** they're ascending were milled from planks salvaged from the original house.

Skip likes to incorporate unexpected blends of old and new in his houses. He sees each old structure as having a forgotten story to tell—a story that slowly reveals itself, out of sequence but legible to the expert craftsmen as they put the pieces back together.

A Walk-In Pantry

MANY PEOPLE REQUEST the luxury of a walk-in pantry when it's time to remodel the kitchen. If designed in the style of "dressed-up utilitarian," a pantry may not have to be a luxury item at all—and might even save a few dollars in the cost of a kitchen remodeling by potentially reducing the number of new cabinets.

The pantry is basically closet storage for dry goods, bulk items, and extra bottled water or soda. It's also a great place to keep the lobster pot and large countertop appliances when they're not in use. Storage on open shelving is adequate, since you can simply close the door if you don't want to see the chaos inside.

Positioning a walk-in pantry depends on the circumstances of your particular home, but generally you'll want to keep it within easy walking distance of the kitchen work areas or convenient to where groceries are brought into the home.

baluster — The vertical pieces of a stair-rail assembly that extend up to the hand rail and form a protective guard.

stringer — A diagonal structural member used to support a stair.

treads — The steps of a stair. The vertical faces between steps are called *risers.*

LEFT, **There is just enough** room at the top of the stairs for a small sitting area near the dormer window. Simplicity is the rule in this 1700s home—square-edged balusters with no adornment make up the rail system, while the shape of the dormer opening and the exposed structural frame add interest to the space without the need for additional molding.

BELOW, **The bedroom walls** follow the slope of the gambrel roof. Dormer windows penetrate the roof at regular intervals and correspond with the location of the collar ties, which are both visually interesting and a structural necessity.

Shaping Your Own World

Well-designed homes can provide us with the opportunity to live better lives. Winston Churchill once said, "We shape our buildings, and thereafter they shape us." Many of us have an undeniable need to shape our own space and to define our own world. And once we've begun, by designing a new home, adding a room off the back, or just remodeling the bathroom, we begin to experience a kind of change. Altering a space can bring a sense of pride, as well as create room for new activities your family may never have tried in a cramped space. Or perhaps opening a room to a new view will encourage you to slow down, and quietly. . .*look*. Once we change the spaces within our homes, we begin to act and react in fresh ways.

The dream phase

Making the decision to build a new home or addition forces you to scrutinize your objectives. Not only do you want to get things right, you also want to avoid costly mistakes along the way. This means lots of hard work. For one, technical competence is required; the building has to physically support itself while keeping the folks within dry and comfortable. Second, there is a necessary sense of order to achieve; the spaces should flow well, have a logical relationship to one another, and satisfy the desired function. Finally, there is an element of style to consider; you have to figure out how to make design decisions that will be aesthetically pleasing and appropriate for you and your region.

But first, allow yourself the enjoyment of a dream phase. You can begin by listing your needs, rather than simply writing down room names, which tends to be too pragmatic. The list should include your *emotional* needs: sunlight, garden views, the sound of water, a

A bright new pair of French doors with a large transom window above admits an abundance of natural light to an otherwise dark entry hall. The increased light draws the owners to the front rooms, encouraging them to use the home's formal spaces on an everyday basis.

sense of openness, a feeling of security, an inspiring place to paint or write, a bustling place where your children can be close by while you prepare the evening meal, a bright space for work and play, or a dark space for deep thought. These items might seem vague or ambiguous, but they will make sense to an architect. The houses rounding out this chapter are examples of how architects have converted the dreams of their clients into functioning, beautiful places to live—all within the framework of Colonial styles.

ADDING ON TO A COLONIAL

The design of even a small addition can be a complex puzzle. As soon as you decide it's time to build a new family room, you'll see the logic of including a new fireplace and maybe a covered place outside for firewood. Quickly, one thing leads to another: Access to the firewood might be easier through a roomy door—maybe a pair of French doors. Why not remove a wall so the view through those doors can be enjoyed from the kitchen? But where will the displaced cupboards go? Maybe a new pantry next to the fridge will take care of that little problem. Or will a pantry block the door to the basement stair? *Gasp!*

If your project threatens to get out of hand like this, it may be time to call on a design professional. An architect who specializes in the tricky quirks and twists of residential projects can solve the problems that come up even in projects of relatively limited scope.

Finding space from within

It costs more to build an addition than to renovate space you already have. If your need for more square footage is modest, start by looking around for a way of shifting an interior wall or changing the role of a couple of rooms. The master bathroom shown in the photo

LEFT, **A home is** a highly personal sanctuary for you and your family and introduces the responsibility to plan carefully—not just for economic good sense, but also for emotional well-being.

FACING PAGE, **This addition** is carefully detailed to mirror the characteristics of the original house while providing its owners with an ample amount of new space.

below grew to nearly twice its size by borrowing a few feet from an adjacent child's bedroom. What this second bedroom lost in square footage was paid back in character—the new partition wall between the two rooms was shaped to form an alcove for a child's desk.

The pluses of adding on

If extra space can't be found inside your Colonial, you'll have to venture outside to meet your needs. An addition will require site work, a foundation, and a building **envelope.** And the new design will have to relate both spatially and visually to the existing home. The Colonial is an orderly, mannered sort of building, and you may want to limit additions on the front to roof dormers,

bay windows, or a new portico. Adding to the sides and back is the recommended way to go if you intend to keep the characteristic Colonial appearance intact. The modest addition shown on the facing page appears as a natural outgrowth of the original house, using the same materials and trim details for an integrated appearance. The new space includes a study and a walk-in closet for the master bedroom above.

The back of a Colonial is *the* place to add on in expressive ways. The owners of the home shown in the top photo on p. 31 enlarged the tiny kitchen of their 1960s suburban Colonial with a sweeping facade and a provocative mix of contemporary and traditional details. Additions out the back introduce interesting

envelope —The collective assembly of the home's floors, walls, and roofs that are exposed to the elements.

This master bathroom is an eclectic blend of new and old. The centrally placed bathtub is the focal point, and the angled partition helps to block the view of the toilet area beyond. Though a new room, it was created by remodeling an existing portion of the house rather than by building an addition.

A new study projects from the side of the main house without interrupting the front facade and roof. Because the addition is visible from the front, it was designed to mimic the formal nature of the public side by repeating the window type, dormer, siding materials, and trim details at the eaves.

Seeking Opportunities on Site

WHENEVER I STEP ONTO a new project site, I'm immediately seeking out opportunities. Sometimes it's obvious—a beautiful view of an adjacent valley or a long vista down a sandy beach. Other positive elements I look for are sun exposure and interesting site features, such as a rock outcropping, a nearby pond, or mature shade trees. In the same way, when you are contemplating a renovation, it's useful to make a site sketch of your property using a survey map as the base sheet, then plot out the desirable features surrounding your home—things worth preserving or taking better advantage of.

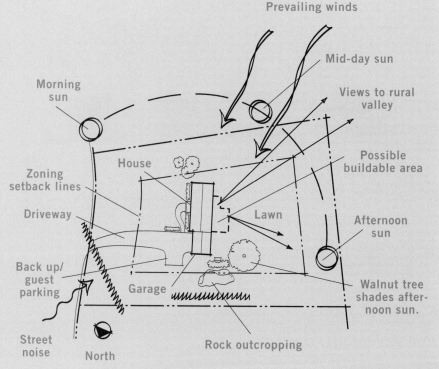

Sample site plan

The basics begin with identifying north and charting the track of the sun. In North America, the sun rises in the east and sets in the west, along an arc that swings south. Draw a big arc on your sketch with a smiling yellow sun at the apex on the south side. Locate your trees, any ponds or streams, your garden, and your play areas. Draw big arrows indicating a distant view, but don't overlook close-up features such as a shade garden adjacent to the house or a swimming pool.

Next, note the location of neighbors and, if you desire privacy, make a big thick line indicating where you'll need to block a view. Note both the prevailing breezes, which can help cool the house, and prevailing winds, which you may want to moderate with a wall or row of greenery as a windbreak. Is your house positioned on a neighborhood street, aligned with other houses? Or is it set back from the road?

Mark the location of the street edge, driveway, and parking areas; if traffic or street noise is an issue, indicate on your sketch where you'd like to block sound or view.

By evaluating your sketch, you'll get an idea of which areas of your addition can be opened up to sunlight, views, and outdoor access to patios and terraces. The map also will suggest ways in which you can have a bit more privacy and insulation from the outside world.

Colonials allow for plenty of creative expression, as in this spirited addition at the back of the house. The new extension defines an exterior space as an outdoor room.

opportunities for outdoor spaces as well. You'll want to consider how your addition shapes these "rooms" as you design. For example, the area to the side of this kitchen created a spot for a sunny deck.

RENOVATIONS: LIBERATING YOUR OLDER COLONIAL

Renovating gives you the opportunity to redirect the language of your home while staying put in a neigh-borhood you've grown to love. Of course, it also can be the time for strictly practical matters, such as replacing the roof, updating plumbing fixtures, and adding spark to your heating system. Following are examples that show how homeowners have expressed themselves by reworking their houses. You'll find ideas on gaining and altering space so that your Colonial can function in a more satisfying way.

Carefully conceived details help this addition to marry with the original house, constructed 150 years prior. A comprehensive renovation often includes both remodeling the original house and putting on an addition or two, improving a quirky floor plan while increasing living area.

Strategic planning

Renovation is an all-inclusive phrase for an all-inclusive process. In the renovation shown in the bottom photo on p. 31, the owners not only cleaned up some old trouble spots but also doubled the floor area with a series of smaller additions that prevent the home from appearing overly large.

In a renovation of a different kind, shown below, the project stayed closer to the concepts of architectural preservation, selectively blending in the owners' own ideas as they worked on their 1694 Saltbox. The family can now enjoy the convenience of a modern lifestyle while surrounded by a home that honors a time long past, complete with a remarkable collection of Early American art, artifacts, and antiques.

You may wish to stay with the style of your house when renovating and enlarging for a consistent, unified appearance—or you may choose to venture into new territory. In the Colonial shown on p. 35, differing styles come together to create a bold statement. Multiple modern additions were constructed in defiant juxtaposition to the otherwise civil, traditional home. This radical union is made successful by the clarity in which both styles are expressed.

BUILDING A NEW COLONIAL

The luster of age attracts us to the classics in residential architecture. But many homeowners prefer to start a Colonial house from scratch. By building a new home, you can avoid the quirks of odd plan arrangements,

LEFT, **This Early American** home underwent a thorough renovation. The difficult chore of integrating electrical wiring and other modern conveniences had to be overcome to retain its distinctive historic spirit.

FACING PAGE, **Make your new house** a good neighbor by choosing a Colonial style that's appropriate for the region where you plan to build. The essence of another era comes across in this brand-new coastal home. It reflects the nautical surroundings with the placement of a widow's walk atop the roof.

LEFT, **Many of us like** both sides of the architectural coin; modern principles can be connected with traditional ideals in exciting ways to create homes of unequaled distinction.

FACING PAGE, **Twin gables embrace** a bold gesture of welcome in a home that defies conventional design. Renovating isn't just replacing old siding and a worn roof—it can also be an opportunity to give the home new direction and meaning.

Focus on Your Colonial Renovation

RENOVATION WILL REJUVENATE a house and make it more enjoyable. And a well-planned renovation can be an outstanding investment. But most of us have to limit the scope of our projects, choosing to improve those parts of the house that will have the most impact. Where should you start?

Real estate agents identify the kitchen and the master bathroom as the most seriously scrutinized spaces by prospective buyers. If a Colonial has appliances, cabinets, faucets, tile, and even towel bars from 20 or 30 years ago, the entire home may feel stale. If possible, go beyond replacing these details and get an architect's fresh thinking on altering the floor plan to improve the quality of life at home.

Ranking a close second to these areas are casual living spaces and additional bedrooms. Today, most everyone prefers a large family room with comfortable seating where multiple activities can occur at once. Family spaces should have good natural light and access to a nearby terrace or patio. Consider adding a bedroom if you have fewer than four—the benchmark number throughout most of the nation. The minimum acceptable floor area for a guest or children's room is about 12 ft. by 12 ft. While adding a bedroom can pay off at resale time, *enlarging* a child's bedroom is thought to reap little return on your investment dollar.

aching mechanical equipment, and the uncertainty of expensive secrets hidden behind walls. And of course the big advantage of building a new home is the freedom to design a house to suit your own very particular needs on your own very particular site.

In designing a new Colonial home, you'll want to consider its style in relation to the region of the country where you plan to build. For example, Spanish Colonials are a poor fit in the Northeast and, likewise, a Federal reproduction would look out of place in the arid Southwest. A house must make a proper fit with its location or it will seem gimmicky rather than rooted.

Substance over size

Although new houses continue to be built with the square footage of palaces, there seems to be a healthy trend toward smaller homes that are designed with interesting spaces and lovingly crafted details. Architect Robert Reed's Washington home (see the photo on p. 36) is only about 2,000 sq. ft., but its versatile rooms allow a dressed-up look for a formal dinner party while also comfortably supporting the family's everyday activities. The intelligently sized home was economical to construct, using far less lumber than the average contemporary Colonial, and the compact well-insulated envelope is economical to heat.

By designing fewer rooms that will be used more often, you can keep the size—and budget—of your new Colonial under control. Open connections between rooms create the illusion of greater space and encourage communication among family members.

If you prefer to have a very large new home, consider a design that spreads the area throughout a main house and a series of smaller masses that have the appearance of additions, rather than risk building a single rectangular structure that will appear overwhelming.

Modern or traditional?

If you find that you feel more alive in homes with wide open spaces, you might consider blending Colonial design with **Modernism.** The bold concepts behind this movement began to brew at the very end of the 1800s and were strongly developed by the 1940s, yet the impact wasn't felt on the suburban homes of the latter date, such as postwar Capes and Colonials. However, several principles of open planning—shared spaces, **layered spaces,** and bright connections to the outdoors—all lend themselves to today's lifestyles and even to the planning of a new Colonial. In Hugh Newell Jacobsen's Florida design (see the photo on p. 34), Modernism intertwines with exterior forms and materials symbolic of traditional architecture. Once inside, the interior is absent of any ornamentation or applied decoration—another attribute of the movement.

Even if you choose to construct a new Colonial that stands as a sentimental tribute to past styles, you can benefit from open planning principles that will allow you to live more comfortably with less space. Open arrangements let the family stay in sight of one another while the kids watch TV, Dad fixes dinner, and Mom analyzes the closing stock figures on the Internet. In a new Colonial you can look forward to blending historic meaning with lessons from contemporary architecture.

☆ Williamsburg—The Colonial Capital

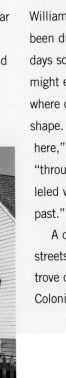

THERE'S NO BETTER PLACE to see Colonial architecture at its finest than in the remarkable living museum located in Williamsburg, Virginia. The capital city of the largest and wealthiest colony while under English rule, Williamsburg survived both the Revolutionary War and the Civil War mostly unscathed, only to be swallowed whole by commercial development. In 1926, the restoration of the former Colonial capital began under the direction of visionary Dr. W.A.R. Goodwin with financial backing provided by industrial tycoon and philanthropist John D. Rockefeller. Goodwin's dream was to preserve Williamsburg as it had been during its halcyon days so that all Americans might experience the place where our republic took shape. "There are windows here," he explained, "through which unparalleled vistas open into the nation's past."

A day spent strolling the streets can provide a treasure trove of ideas for your own Colonial home. Details we've either lost to time or have entirely taken for granted appear fresh again—functioning window shutters on iron hardware, clever decorative cuts on exterior trim, and an amazing variety of fences and garden gates.

Modernism ⌐ An architectural movement most active from 1900 to 1940, including such styles as Prairie, Art Moderne, Art Deco, and International.

layered spaces ⌐ The unfolding or overlapping of several spaces that are moderately open to one another, each offering a preview of the next.

ABOVE AND FACING PAGE, **Although varying tastes** in style and decoration set us apart, the need for shelter and desire for physical and emotional well-being within our homes is shared by everyone. The Colonial has provided such a setting for well over 300 years.

AN AMERICAN EVOLUTION

The best of the old seems to be making a comeback in neighborhoods across the country, and Colonial homes are attracting an impressive number of homebuyers. Owners of new and renovated Colonials enjoy the ability to enrich their everyday lives through new architecture that is really *old* architecture. Those who take the initiative to reconstruct a centuries-old home are helping to perpetuate the historic ribbon of American architecture. An outdated home can be reworked to accommodate a contemporary lifestyle. And the construction of an all-new home in this vital, steadfast style takes advantage of a design legacy going back centuries. After all, current architectural ideas are not the product of some newly invented age—they are part of an evolution. In the

Architects and homebuyers have reawakened to the virtues of Colonial house types, with their unparalleled design legacy. Today, expectations go beyond mere square footage. The owners of these time-honored houses seek well-planned family and entertainment spaces and meaningful details anchored within the spirit of an earlier time.

1600s, the early settlers of Virginia and Massachusetts constructed timber homes resembling the architecture of their homelands, and they found emotional security by building what seemed familiar. Today, 350 years later, it is entirely remarkable that, even though we can choose from a palette of thousands of building materials, we continue to take comfort in these snug, sensible homes.

Each of the Colonial homes in this book has an interesting story to tell. We'll look at new homes, renovated homes, and homes with modest additions. They are big and little, modern and antique. I hope that your own wishes and dreams for a Colonial home will come a little closer to being realized as you page through the chapters ahead.

CHAPTER TWO

REMODELING MODESTLY

A welcome addition for busy families: a mudroom at the back door with plenty of storage nearby. The bench, placed in a small alcove, is a practical place for slipping on shoes and boots.

FOR MANY OF US, RENOVATING AN OUTDATED kitchen or building a new family room out the side may be all that's needed to improve the quality of life at home. Others may require a modestly sized addition for a parent who stays for short-term visits. Maybe an addition containing a study is what's needed for working peacefully at home. Sometimes you can create new rooms without adding on at all; an underused floor plan may already contain enough space for the activities you hope to include in your Colonial.

Whether you're itching for a new playroom for the kids or a sumptuous master suite for yourself, your Colonial can offer clues on finding the best strategy to reach your goals. You simply have to know how and where to look for them.

STRATEGIES FOR ADDING ON

Any number of configurations are possible when it comes to adding new space to a home. Colonials, however, tend to dictate how and where you place an addition and still

When owners of Colonials scan the remodeling horizon, their eyes most frequently light on the kitchen. The traditional appeal of this new country-style kitchen is enhanced with the installation of grouped windows, which lets the light pour in and creates virtual elbow room for the cozy table setting.

The second-floor expansion of this bedroom took advantage of the sloped roof for a cathedral ceiling and a tall Palladian-inspired window. The ceiling was clad in wood with a V-groove edge for a refined texture, then brightly painted to reflect light.

box window — A grouping of windows that projects outward from the exterior wall of the home in a rectilinear shape, like a box.

bay window — A grouping of windows, with angled sidewalls, that projects outward from the exterior wall of the home.

end up with a home that looks like a Colonial. The answer frequently is in the form of an addition that extends out one side, both sides, or out the back. If your Colonial already has a single-story appendage poking out somewhere, you may be able to add a new bathroom or a bedroom by building a second floor on top.

Adding out

A Colonial home tends to look best if the main house stays in the forefront. If you or your architect decide that an addition positioned to the side is appropriate, you'll want to ensure that it steps back enough so the front facade remains prominent. This strategy can cost you less as well, by avoiding the expense of trying to match up siding and roofing. Commonly, additions to the front are limited to expanding the entry hall, constructing a new portico, or adding **box** or **bay windows,** the last two being closer to "details" than an addition.

Adding informal rooms to the back of the house has created many a successful addition, leaving the formal spaces such as the living and dining rooms undisturbed at the front. This arrangement makes sense—at the back of the house you can be less concerned about the rigor of the style. If you've ever felt the front of your Colonial is a little like a dinner jacket, then let the back be the Hawaiian shirt and have some fun. In the privacy of your own backyard, you can feel free to open up walls to banks of tall windows, vary roof lines, or add a garden arbor over the kitchen window.

Adding up

Adding on to the first floor can economically satisfy the need for space on the second floor as well. You may want to consider building a new bedroom or enlarging

Spanish Colonial Hallmarks

WHEN THE SPANISH COLONIZED Florida and the American Southwest, they brought with them an architecture that combined the traditions of their homeland and the vernacular shelters of Native Americans. These dwellings were far different from the early English-derived houses. The walls were of stone or adobe brick and coated with a protective layer of mud or plaster to seal the structure from the elements. The construction was solid and thick—it had to be to support its own weight—and absorbed the heat of the sun by day, then radiated it back into rooms for warmth on chilly nights. The walls had small openings for light and ventilation, guarded by wood bars and wood shutters; glass simply was not available.

Early Spanish dwellings had simple rectangular plans of one to three rooms wide. The style later developed into a sprawling courtyard scheme, with several rooms surrounding a garden patio, or *placita*.

This provided a refreshing oasis in the hot climate, accessible from the entire house.

Roofs typically were low-pitched, capped with familiar half-round Spanish tiles. A porch, or *portale*, was a common feature, supported by simple timber posts and beams, or by grand, arched colonnades in finer homes.

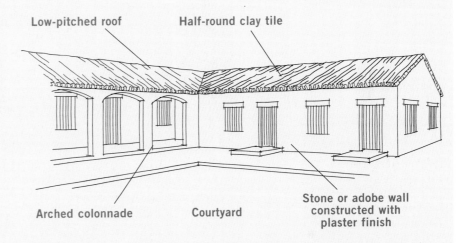

Low-pitched roof   Half-round clay tile

Arched colonnade   Courtyard   Stone or adobe wall constructed with plaster finish

In time, the Spanish designs showed the influence of other styles, and Baroque and Greek Revival versions now account for most of what we recognize as Spanish Colonial architecture.

the master suite as you prepare to design the spaces below. Unfortunately, the spaces you might hope to build upstairs seldom align perfectly with those on the bottom, so be prepared to call in an architect for creative problem solving, because the planning of a two-story addition can sometimes be tricky.

Your home may already have a single-story addition, giving you the opportunity to build above. If the existing foundation is suitable for such an expansion,

it might be a ready-made solution for an extra bathroom, a sewing room, or an art space for the kids. Make sure the design of a new second-floor room or expansion doesn't block or force the removal of indispensable windows in any upstairs bedrooms. Bedroom window sizes are regulated by the building code for emergency egress in case of a fire—and every bedroom needs at least a window or two for light and ventilation.

ABOVE, **The addition steps** back from the side of this Colonial to keep the emphasis on the main house. This design strategy also simplifies construction because there is no need to exactly mate the original roofing and front siding with new materials.

RIGHT, **This extra room** is nestled beneath the sloping roof of an attached garage. The openings for the dormer windows dramatically pierce the sloped ceiling, improve headroom along the low sides, and provide additional floor space.

drop ⁀ A decorative pendant carved or cut from wood.

Old spaces with new uses

Some Colonials have the luxury of a spatial surplus. Assigning a new function to an unused room can be a relatively painless way to satisfy your quest for new space. To enlarge the kitchen, could you expand into a portion of a seldom-used formal dining room? Connecting the rooms by removing the shared wall will encourage you to use the space more often. Or, you might divide a lengthy Colonial living room to create a library on one side and a small sitting area on the other. Keep in mind the formal and informal areas of your Colonial when planning, and place new rooms next to those that are most compatible. If you need a quiet study, for example, it might be better suited alongside the living room rather than the family room, with the distractions of a flickering television and a dozen activities. Likewise, an active family room is best positioned next to the kitchen rather than across the house where it may feel isolated.

Many older Colonials have screened porches placed off of the living room or formal dining room, which can be awkward if you often serve meals out there: imagine balancing a tippy platter of saucy ribs as you walk over a good carpet and past fine furniture. If you strive to mate the formal spaces with formal spaces and the informal spaces with their own kind, you'll enjoy a better functioning floor plan (and avoid messy jobs such as stain removal).

Expressive details can elevate a plain Colonial above the ordinary. These twin balconies make a personal statement and unify the existing structure at the left with a new addition.

The little details that count

Architecture speaks a language—not with words, but with built pieces that form symbols. Many of the clients who approach my firm feel their homes don't tell the story of who they really are. Through the use of meaningful details, you can successfully transform your house into a home expressive of you and your family. In the home shown below, a pair of balconies with curving brackets and decorative **drops** set this addition apart from the ordinary. The garage door at the left is original to the house, while the other doors are part of the addition. Above the expanded garage is a new laundry room and exercise room.

A feature that owners of Colonials often add to give their homes more personality is an entry portico. Colonial facades are generally flat, without weather protection at the central front door. Adding a roofed porch the full length of the front facade might unintentionally

cut off natural light to the front rooms. The more compact portico is a reliable design solution, offering a gracious expression of welcome while protecting family and guests who arrive during a rain storm.

Entry porticos on Colonials tend to lean toward the classical, with round columns supporting an **entablature** and **pediment** above. A good builder with an understanding of classical design can create a portico for you, but you may want to enlist the help of an architect who has plenty of experience with this somewhat complicated detailing. If you prefer a portico with a whimsical or expressive twist, you may get the most interesting and abstract variation from an architect who is experienced in designing *perfectly* in the classical manner. An example of a classical portico designed with such creative license is around the corner from the twin balconies shown on p. 45. Architect Charles Emerson created a portico with a triangular roof, supported at the tip by a single column, to accommodate a walkway with a diagonal approach to the house (see the photo on the facing page).

Modest and manageable

It can be exhilarating to realize the possibilities in adding on to your home's footprint. Even a modest addition can provide a marked improvement to the floor plan, allowing your home to function as though you really added much more.

The owners of the home shown on p. 49 chose a modest and manageable approach when they added a study on the first floor and a master bathroom directly above. Their plot of land is expansive and sunny, and they felt the new rooms should capture that feeling. As a result, the new spaces have large windows that admit plenty of natural light and frame a view across the rolling lawn. The study takes further advantage of the outdoors by offering convenient access to the back terrace through a single French door. The rear of the study has a covered porch supported by columns to protect the room from the afternoon's hot, western sun. Upstairs, an oversized bathtub is positioned alongside large windows for a view while taking a soak.

entablature ⌒ A classical lintel supported by columns.

pediment ⌒ The closed, triangular-shaped gable of a classical structure.

Memory makers such as this garden bench, recessed within a stone foundation wall, create opportunities to enjoy our homes more thoroughly and to inspire our imaginations.

Colonial facades are generally flat and lack a sheltering canopy, or portico, at the front door. This intriguing addition, with a single, central column, is triangular in shape to meet an angled approach from the driveway.

The trim details surrounding the front doors of older Colonials give us clues to discover the historic period during which the home was constructed. This example, with a lofty arched transom is a Federal period or Adam Style Colonial.

awning window—An operable swinging window that is hinged at the top.

The addition shown in the photo on p. 51 takes another approach to making the most of a small space by including backyard views and admitting an abundance of light. An impressive bank of windows opens this sunroom to the outdoors. The grouping of square **awning windows** has a small-scale charm and plenty of visual interest with its crisscross grid of narrow muntins and hefty mullions.

The owners cheerfully admit that the design of the sunroom is topped only by their new kitchen (shown in the photo on p. 50). This stylish work area was designed for gourmet meal preparation as well as the occasional PB & J. The plan provides the couple with a highly efficient work zone placed between two islands. This prep space is defined by four columns placed at the outer ends of the islands. It's a spot where friends

Arriving at Your Front Door

VARIATIONS

☆ **THE ENTRY DOOR** is the most important spot on the front of your home. It is the main point of arrival, the place where you greet friends and guests—and it's a barrier against unwanted visitors. A wood door expresses quality and sets the tone for the place you call home.

A 1¾-in.-thick raised-panel wood door is the standard type for most Colonials. But I often recommend a custom 2¼-in.-thick door when it's time for a replacement—not necessarily for strength, but for the tactile sense. The heft and feel of a thick door add a substantiveness to your dwelling. A popular design for Colonial homes has six panels. You can choose to replace the top two solid panels with glass panes, which will admit a little extra daylight into the entry hall. A unique alternative is a four-panel door with the tall, thin panels oriented vertically.

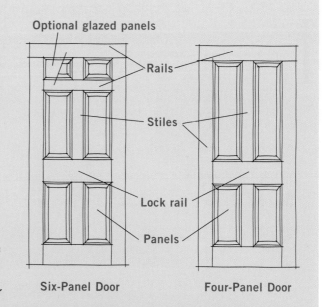

Optional glazed panels
Rails
Stiles
Lock rail
Panels

Six-Panel Door   Four-Panel Door

and family can gather around to chat or just watch. Lengthy counters are positioned perpendicular to the island area, offering convenient stations for additional cooks and plenty of cabinets for storage.

The curving vault above the kitchen adds spatial volume and a sense of connection between the work space and the nearby table area. The vault draws your eye to an arched window positioned over a wall of double-hung windows and a single French door leading to a wood deck. The interesting details don't stop here—at the opposite end of the vault, a tapered steel hood, suspended from above by stainless-steel rods, acts as a dramatic sculptural piece while providing the necessary ventilation for the heavy-duty commercial cooktop.

As you examine the projects ahead and begin the planning of your own addition, try and think beyond

ABOVE, **The upper windows** on the gable end of this two-story addition are boxed out slightly for visual interest.

LEFT, Inside, the extra depth of the box makes a convenient shelf at the sill. The custom windows tilt in at the top to admit fresh air, and with the twist of a handle, they operate as casements to maximize ventilation.

A vaulted ceiling follows the arc of the upper window in this luminous, airy kitchen. Beneath the arched window, a wall of glass provides generous views from the kitchen's primary work zone. The door between the lower windows makes for quick access to the deck and barbecue.

Planning and Zoning

☆ PRACTICAL MATTERS

YOUR NEIGHBORHOOD IS CATEGORIZED within your community into a zoning district. It's important to find out which zoning district your home sits within prior to the planning of your project by visiting the local planning and zoning department. You'll also need a survey map that shows your house on the property, or simply the property boundaries if you have a bare lot. If you don't have a copy or can't find one in the records room of your town hall, you'll need to hire a licensed professional surveyor to create one for you.

With survey in hand, ask your planning and zoning official to provide you with detailed information regarding your particular zoning district. You'll want to make sure your addition or new home fits within the property line setbacks, does not exceed the allowable lot coverage (or the allowable floor area ratio), and does not exceed any height restrictions. Describe your project to the official and see if he or she has any advice for you. For example, expanding your kitchen or family room might involve a routine check of property line setbacks and lot coverage. But a separate guest house might require a public hearing, site plan approval, and a special permit.

mere economy or utility. Strive for well-designed spaces and interesting, meaningful details—a home can be transformed by even small gestures. The additions and interior remodelings that you'll see all sprang from solid planning and are brimming with inspiring details. These projects are attainable in scope and are powerful in the enlivening effect on the homes they grace.

This casual addition at the back of the home is brightened with numerous awning windows arranged in a basic geometric composition. When all of the windows are open, the room takes on the feel of a screened porch.

A Study in Logic

This addition enjoys plenty of ventilation, natural light, and views to a private side yard. The gable-end window is surrounded by smooth horizontal siding in textural contrast with the clapboard below.

builder's Colonial —Refers to post-World War II Colonials constructed generally from stock plans, often for the speculative housing market.

N
EW COLONIAL HOMES BUILT FROM STOCK plans tend to suffer from similar design problems and are often ready for a logical reorganizing before the moving truck is even out of the driveway. After living only a year in this **builder's Colonial,** Ken and Patricia asked an architect for help. They wanted to add on a small study, dress up the family room which was spacious but lacking in interior details, and redesign the kitchen which was in the main path of traffic between the family room and the other areas of the home.

FOCUSING ON WHAT WORKS

The owners were anxious to set these things right, but they cringed at the thought of throwing away a nearly new, perfectly good batch of kitchen cabinets, natural stone countertops, and appliances. The architect came up with a thrifty design that allowed these components to be reused without compromising the new layout. They also decided that an access to a nearby terrace would be welcome, but the cabinets blocked the only wall where an exterior door could be installed. The solution came by flipping the entire kitchen, carefully removing, and then reinstalling the cabinets on the interior wall. The granite countertops were gently lifted and sent to a stoneyard for recutting. The wall facing

The rich tones of this room are brightened by a grouping of tall casement windows. The window alcove makes room for extra seating.

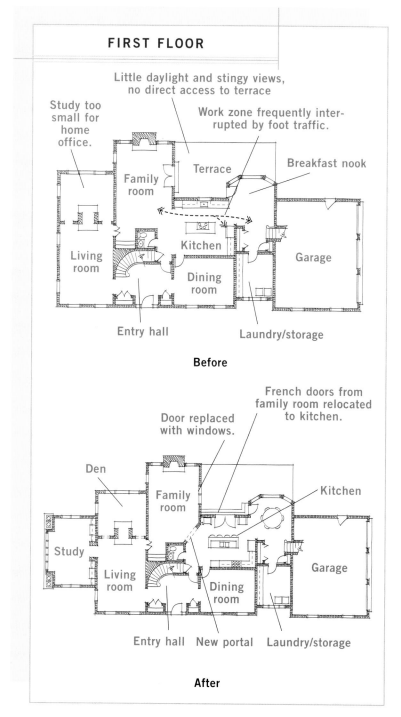

FIRST FLOOR

Study too small for home office.

Little daylight and stingy views, no direct access to terrace

Work zone frequently interrupted by foot traffic.

Family room

Terrace

Breakfast nook

Living room

Kitchen

Garage

Dining room

Entry hall

Laundry/storage

Before

Door replaced with windows.

French doors from family room relocated to kitchen.

Den

Family room

Kitchen

Study

Living room

Garage

Dining room

Entry hall   New portal   Laundry/storage

After

the terrace was now free to install French doors with a **transom,** and tall pantry cabinets to either side. Not only does the remodeled kitchen function better but additional storage was created and natural light and views to the back make the space a much more enjoyable place to work and socialize.

DEVELOPING CONTINUITY THROUGH DETAILS

The remodeled kitchen was visible from the family room, and the new study was just a short walk from there. A thread was needed that would tie these spaces together so the rooms wouldn't end up feeling like an unrelated set of abrupt experiences. A palette of fresh trim details based on traditional profiles was introduced to create the necessary unity. The corners of the cherry kitchen island are emphasized with a fluting detail that is repeated in a new passage to the family room, where the unadorned drywall walls of the kitchen blandly turned a corner (see the photo on p. 57). The lack of any emphasis in this place of transition created the unsettling effect of not knowing where one room ended and the other began. Without sacrificing the openness between the two spaces, the passage, or "portal," better defines each space and actually links the two rooms, underscoring their inseparable relationship.

A second portal between the living room and the new study was constructed to further emphasize the continuity of the design. The portals don't match precisely. In fact, they're quite opposite when it comes to styling, visual weight, and even symbolic meaning. In the casual atmosphere of the family room, the painted

transom — A source of light or ventilation from over a door.

ABOVE, **This passage that leads** to the
new study is dark and solid, suggesting
the private nature of the space.

LEFT, **Wainscot paneling** in the family
room shares details with the cherry island
in the nearby kitchen, creating a harmonious continuity of style.

The kitchen renovation made use of the existing cabinets and stone countertops. The island is a new U-shaped enclosure of cherry, fitted with the salvaged sink cabinet, drawer stack, and dishwasher.

LEFT, **An eyebrow dormer** window admits a sliver of natural light from high above. Unusual for a Colonial home, the eyebrow shape adds a whimsical touch inside and out.

BELOW, **The new portal** simultaneously separates and links the kitchen and family room. Though highly custom in its appearance, the portal is assembled with standard molding profiles, available at any lumberyard.

portal with its open transom appears light and welcoming. Entering the study, one notes that the solid mahogany passageway is narrower, darker, and deeper, signaling a private area of the home.

The study is a work-at-home office for Ken and needed lots of storage for books, electronic gear, and a computer. Long bookcases on either side of the portal swallow nearly all the owner needs to store. The woodwork travels around the room in the tradition of an old library. An alcove filled with tall windows floods the room with light and shows off the dark, rich wood tones (see the photo on p. 53). This cozy nook, only 2 ft. in depth, is more than sufficient to hold a small table and a pair of club chairs for watching the news or casual conferencing.

Ken and Patricia have given their new home an early second chance and are now prepared for many years of enjoyment in new and remodeled rooms created especially to suit their tastes. Large, recently built homes with planning conflicts and stark interiors are an unfortunate reality for many new owners. But an uninspired design can be overcome with a thoughtfully planned reworking that shows an appreciation for small details.

Room for Sharing

ABOVE, **Peace of mind** is a call away—an intercom in the sleeping area and also in a nearby bathroom keep an extended family under one roof in touch with each other.

FACING PAGE, **The addition** to the left of the new entry door contains a comfortable suite for an elderly parent. The window openings toward the street are small to cut down on unwanted noise.

INCREASINGLY, HOMEOWNERS ARE ASKING architects to develop spaces within their homes for an elderly parent. Sometimes it's a financial necessity. But largely the choice is to integrate an older generation under the same roof where both have much to offer. And it's an opportunity for capable, grown children to return the love and nurturing their parents afforded them in earlier years.

Designing for an elderly parent involves several special considerations in terms of accessibility, safety, and comfort. Richard and Diane turned to our firm when they decided it was time for Richard's mother, Kathryn, to move into their 1960s Colonial. Kathryn was approaching her 80th birthday. Her vision was impaired and she had lost some mobility, but she was able to move around with the help of a walker. Richard and Diane wanted her to have a comfortable suite with a private bathroom, kitchenette, sitting area, and sleeping area. The suite was to be completely accessible to the main house, but it needed to have just enough separation for both the family and Kathryn to have a sense of their own domain.

A DESIGN FOR COMFORT AND ACCESSIBILITY

The family wanted to make sure Kathryn would have enough room to invite friends or family into her private area of the house. At about 20 ft. square, the new suite is large enough to accommodate all of Kathryn's needs, yet smaller than many family rooms in large houses today. A single room incorporates sleeping and living areas with a "floating" partition in the center (see the photo on the facing page). This wall is anchored to the floor, but because it doesn't reach the ceiling, the room seems light and airy. The partial wall helps send the eye over and beyond, emphasizing the entire space and making the room feel larger. It isn't merely a bland room divider but has been neatly finished at the top with a glossy-painted crown molding for an interesting profile.

The partition is placed diagonally for a stimulating, dynamic effect and, to one side, wraps around a kitchenette. The kitchen table is just a few steps away, near tall corner windows for a view of the backyard. The

ABOVE, **The new entry hall** is not only a spacious mudroom but also a buffer between the two living areas. The barrel-shaped stairway leads to a new play room constructed over the existing garage.

RIGHT, **A change in grade** required that two steps be constructed at the new side door entry. But once inside, there are virtually no floor-level changes, allowing freedom of movement for an elderly parent with mobility challenges.

Vivid colors and plenty of light, both natural and artificial, can help compensate for eyesight that isn't as sharp as it once was. The suite has as few doors as possible, easing physical movement from one space to another.

opposite side of the partition provides wall space for Kathryn's bed and night table.

In designing the new suite, we had to anticipate the mobility challenges that Kathryn might have to encounter. For example, we chose to avoid unnecessary doors. The routine act of opening and closing doors can be a difficult task for someone who uses a walker. The partition segregates the space without the need for doors. Of course, there is a door to Kathryn's bathroom, but it is large enough (4 in. wider than the standard 2 ft. 6 in.) to accommodate a wheelchair in the future if necessary. The few doors in the suite have levers, not knobs, because they can be pushed with the fingers or even the wrist rather than having to be gripped and turned—a plus for those with arthritic conditions.

The floor materials were kept flush wherever possible, eliminating projecting thresholds and steps. Even the

exterior deck is flush with the mudroom floor, with a minimal threshold to keep out water. This enables Kathryn to move freely about the house with a minimum of obstructions, including the simple activity of going outside to watch her grandchild playing in the yard.

Because the eyes begin to lose strength and their ability to perceive differences in color beginning around age 50, we specified that approximately 20 percent more lighting than normal should be installed. The lighting can be easily controlled with dimmers should it ever seem too bright. Next, Richard and Diane asked interior designer Elizabeth Schoenherr to select bright colors and fabrics for the interior color scheme. Together, the brilliant lighting and vivid colors are the equivalent of turning up the visual volume a couple of notches, increasing Kathryn's ability to enjoy her environment.

ABOVE, **The rear facade** enjoys a bit of expressive freedom in contrast to the more reserved approach taken at the front of the house.

FACING PAGE, **The absence of** a step at the back door makes it easier to reach the deck for some fresh air. The overhang shelters the door from snow during harsh northeast winters.

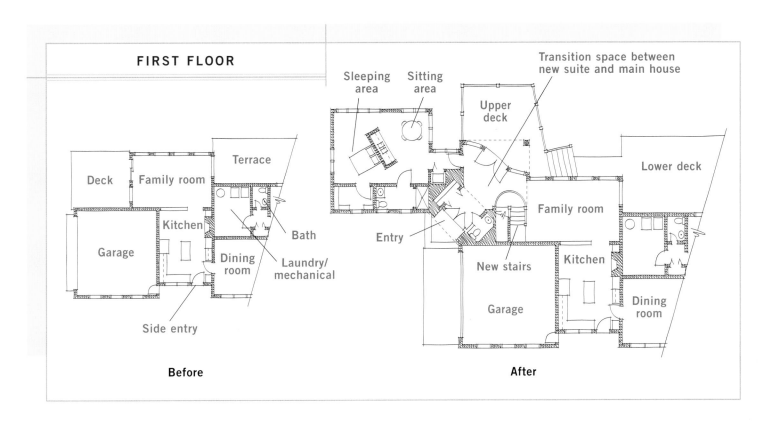

FIRST FLOOR

Deck

Family room

Terrace

Kitchen

Garage

Dining room

Bath

Laundry/mechanical

Side entry

Before

Sleeping area

Sitting area

Transition space between new suite and main house

Upper deck

Lower deck

Family room

Entry

New stairs

Kitchen

Garage

Dining room

After

AN ACROBATIC COMPOSITION OF FORMS

In the completed design, the new side entry serves both as the point of arrival to Kathryn's suite and as a mudroom leading to the kitchen of the main house. The space works as a buffer zone to provide a sense of separation between the two living areas.

Though a rather complicated cluster of new spaces, the addition was organized in a way that exhibits restraint when viewed from the front. At the back of the house the structure is more expressive of the individual functions within, becoming entirely playful. The varied forms are nearly acrobatic in their composition.

The design solution brings a fresh interpretation of the Colonial aesthetic and enlivens the entire house. Notably, the addition retains a residential character inside and out—not an institutional look that some may think is unavoidable. It's no surprise that the many accommodations that were designed specifically for Kathryn's needs make the addition more enjoyable for family and friends as well.

A Fresh Start

ABOVE, **Having been treated** to a new roof, siding, cornerboards, window trim, and porch posts, this modest 1960s Colonial continues to maintain the character of the neighborhood. The heart-pumping changes take place around back.

FACING PAGE, **Lightly toned walls** and bright trim help reflect daylight deep into the interior of the home, lessening the need for supplemental lighting during the day.

T HIS PROJECT IS A PERFECT EXAMPLE of how to solve typical problem areas that confront owners of Colonial homes. Jaki and Brian were no strangers to renovation projects when they spotted a neglected Colonial home for sale on a quiet, tree-lined street. The couple had recently completed the remodeling of a small beach house in a nearby waterfront community but eventually decided to sell because of the traffic and lack of parking. They set their sights on the rural atmosphere of neighborhoods farther inland and found a home that could give them a fresh start.

The 1960s Colonial Jaki and Brian purchased was more spacious than their previous home, but the floor plan and the condition of the house were less than ideal. In fact, it seemed that every plus to their new home came with a corresponding negative point. The yard was spacious and had an in-ground pool, but access from the house was limited. The Colonial had a formal dining room, something their beach house was missing, but the kitchen was dark and had never been updated. Other areas of the house were simply worn out; the siding and roof had become badly deteriorated, a small deck to the rear of the house was derelict, and the landscaping was either overgrown or nonexistent. Working with their architect, the couple set out to make their new home as special as it could possibly be.

LEFT, **A new addition** to the kitchen breaks from traditional notions of Colonial architecture, yet the home maintains a hint of the old style through the use of wood-muntined windows and abstracted features such as the classically inspired entablature and pilasters.

FACING PAGE, **The new kitchen can accommodate** many activities at once—at the primary work area, the prep sink, the island, and the peninsula.

The new addition and deck are framed by an architecturally sassy gesture—a curving, abstract entablature. This bold element invigorates an otherwise demure facade.

CLEANING UP OLD LINES

Jaki and Brian drew on their spartan sensibility for the home's new direction. They preferred simple lines over complicated patterns—crisp and clean instead of fussy and fancy. They wanted easy access to the yard and pool and also *visual* access so they could enjoy the view of their wooded suburban setting.

To take advantage of the site, the architect introduced a large deck for seating, socializing, and dining. This gave the family a new outdoor room, with a wide stair that leads down to the lawn. Over the stair, a gracefully curving classical entablature springs from the rear of the house and forms a gateway to the backyard. Dubbed the "Wandering Arbor" by the architects, the soaring portal forms an S curve as it stretches across the facade of the new kitchen and then outward across the top of the stair. The abstracted classical detailing and the bold nature of the design combine in a surprisingly successful way to help unite this Colonial home with the twenty-first century.

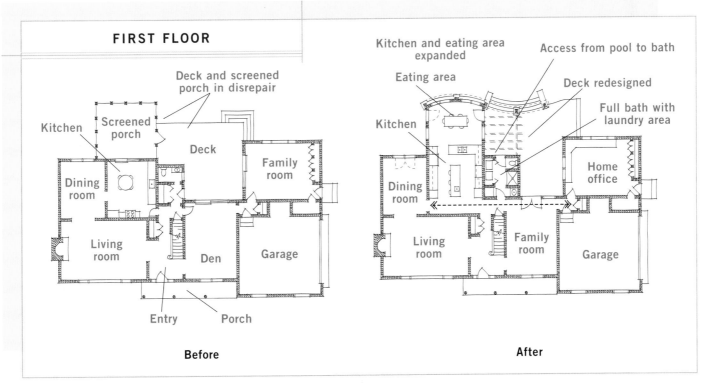

FIRST FLOOR

Deck and screened porch in disrepair

Kitchen

Screened porch

Deck

Family room

Dining room

Living room

Den

Garage

Entry

Porch

Before

Kitchen and eating area expanded

Access from pool to bath

Eating area

Deck redesigned

Kitchen

Full bath with laundry area

Dining room

Home office

Living room

Family room

Garage

After

ABOVE, **The new bathroom** can be accessed by swimmers without traversing through the house. A wood trellis helps make the transition between the outside and the interior. Privacy for the bathroom is controlled with a simple louvered shade attached to the French door.

BELOW, **Colonial doesn't mean cluttered.** The owners preferred a crisp, clean aesthetic over fussy or fancy. The result is a quiet elegance that doesn't rely on ornamentation.

circulation — The areas in a home where we walk, the traffic zones.

STRAIGHTENING A FEW PLANNING KINKS

Jaki and Brian's requirements for the project included a spacious kitchen where the family could socialize with friends, an informal eating area for everyday meals, a bathroom accessible from the pool, and an improved approach from the family room to the deck and backyard. To arrange these new areas logically, they first had to straighten a few kinks in the **circulation.** Properly designed traffic areas make the difference between a floor plan that really works and one that fights you every step of the way. To satisfy this problem, a distinct central hall was developed, stretching nearly the length of the main floor and linking the new and remodeled spaces with the existing plan.

Jaki and Brian emphasized the importance their new kitchen would hold for them. They wanted enough room to accommodate the entire family handily, even if

Light Up the Night

KITCHENS ARE PLEASURABLE SPOTS to socialize in. Every party starts and ends up in the kitchen. And children love to hang around a parent who is preparing a cup of hot chocolate or the evening meal. Reward your admiring onlookers, and yourself, with stylish and functional lighting that goes beyond the common recessed ceiling "can."

General lighting, placed in or on the ceiling, should be adequate to light the whole of the kitchen space during meal preparation and cleanup. In addition to such obvious choices as recessed lighting, you can also consider a close-to-ceiling fixture—that is, a fixture with a decorative glass diffuser mounted relatively tight to the surface of the ceiling.

Task lighting is essential to work efficiently—and safely, especially when handling sharp knives. Low-pro-file, under-cabinet lighting can illuminate your busiest work areas while staying neatly out of view.

Accent lighting delivers a controlled beam of light to highlight interesting features or objects in a room. It's also well suited for counters with casual seating. You can bring the source of light over counter areas to nearly eye level by using a pendant fixture with a glass shade. There are many styles of decorative pendants to choose from, with colorful (or colorless) glass diffusers. Use a light switch with a dimmer to control the intensity of the lighting to suit the attitude of the evening.

they were involved in a variety of different activities. The kitchen was to be a center for the children's homework and craft projects, including novice baking endeavors and meal preparation. The couple also anticipated entertaining a fair number of friends, and they knew all too well that every party seems to wind up in the kitchen. A new island, warmly lit with a trio of sophisticated lighting fixtures, has become a great place for early arrivals to hang out with the hosts until the festivities kick into high gear.

PRACTICAL POOL ACCESS

Anyone who has a swimming pool knows how much clutter is created after a swimming session. When it's time to towel off, Jaki can direct her children across the deck and into quarters designed for a water-logged crew. This versatile area contains a full bathroom, towel and toy storage, and best of all, a full laundry room.

Jaki established a summer theme by selecting soothing water shades of aqua and teal, together with stainless-steel fixtures and fittings for a clean, tropical look. The French door further emphasizes the connection to sunshine and outdoor living. Jaki installed a retractable blind to create privacy.

The renovation of this suburban home is relatively modest: It boils down to a new kitchen and bath, some fiddling with the floor plan, and attention to maintenance items such as the roof and siding. From the street, the home is conventional and remains a good fit with the surrounding neighbors, while the transformation to the rear is striking, with a fun approach expressive of family life.

Capturing Character

ABOVE, **Several additions** and outbuildings come together to create the character of a rambling Yankee farmstead. The connecting link maintains a low profile, nicely setting off the two-story addition at the left.

FACING PAGE, **The loft above** contains the owner's study. Below are spaces that can benefit from a lower ceiling: the bathroom and the closets. The stair leading up to the study saves on space by using pie-shaped steps called winders.

THE ADDITION TO THE HOME featured in pp. 64–69 is a successful departure from the existing house, but many homeowners prefer to stay within the hallmarks of the Colonial type. Carol and Chris asked architect David Barbour to design an addition that would gain them new space for a master bedroom suite and a new study, while sharing a common link with the main house, constructed in the late 1700s. David met the couple's goals by creating a discrete wing that extends laterally from the original home and captures the character of an earlier era.

The addition and the connecting link fit right in, thanks to the use of such traditional materials as clapboard, muntined windows, and classical trim. By turning the gable toward the street, David created a pleasing variation of roof lines. Historically, an attached barn would be positioned in this manner, and the addition's silhouette does look like a barn; but the refined exterior materials and the Palladian-inspired windows indicate unmistakably that this is an extension of interior living space, not quarters for livestock.

A simple passageway links the two parts of the house, acting as a buffer and retaining the integrity of the original structure. This arrangement is in keeping with the rambling character common among traditional New England Colonial farmsteads.

ABOVE, **This home's new addition,** with a study and a master bedroom, takes the appearance of an attached barn. The link creates separation between the old and the new, preserving the integrity of the 1700s Colonial home.

RIGHT, **A mudroom added during** the remodeling provides a transition area between the outdoors and interior—a space preceding the other rooms of the home with a durable floor surface and storage for coats and shoes.

A Well-Structured Environment

Carol and Chris's master bedroom reaches upward to a sloped ceiling and reveals a structural frame of carefully assembled reclaimed timber (see the photo on p. 75). The space is airy and modern yet constructed with traditional materials and age-old techniques.

Inside and out, it's easy to draw similarities to a barn (albeit with more civilized inhabitants). The study is located in a loft overlooking the sleeping area and is accessed by a staircase with space-saving pie-shaped treads called **winders.** Positioned to one end of the addition, the loft creates an area with a low ceiling over closets and the master bathroom, something like stalls beneath a hayloft.

Working For Scale

Clients sometimes tell me that cathedral ceilings leave them feeling cold and even a little vulnerable. In many newer homes, those soaring spaces may be drywall smooth and absent of color, while the walls are timidly adorned with undersized art and decoration. Carol and Chris's bedroom, on the other hand, seems much more inviting because of the timber frame. It brings a sense of scale, referenced by the size of our own bodies. Few of us think much about scale or realize its continual effect on our psyche as we move through the built environment. But its impact is noticeable enough that we feel cold in too-tall spaces, humbled by grand cathedrals, intimidated by the massive Neoclassical facades of public buildings, vulnerable in vast urban plazas, caged in an elevator, or perfectly cozy in an inglenook by a crackling fire. In Carol and Chris's bedroom, the stout horizontal timbers imply the presence of a ceiling floating just overhead, making this room intimate and a comfortable place to relax.

The link provides a preview of what's to come in the addition—a timber frame typical of homes built in the 1700s and early 1800s.

winders — Pie-shaped stair treads used to continue the climb while turning a corner.

A new dining room is set against the backdrop of what was formerly the home's exterior wall. By keeping the old materials intact, the room takes on the casual character of a country farmhouse.

DINNER IN A SPECIAL PLACE

Carol and Chris tapped into the Yankee method of creating a "random" addition when it was time to build a new dining room. This space was logically connected with the kitchen and the living room. The couple chose to keep the old doors, windows, and exterior siding in place as an interesting feature. It's not left to anyone's imagination as to where the back wall of the house used to be! And the sheer novelty of the unique backdrop is a nice foil to the formality of a conventional dining room.

Another clever feature of the dining room is an inward step at both outside corners, allowing a slender window to be added in the niche (see the photo on p. 77). This has the effect of disconnecting the outer

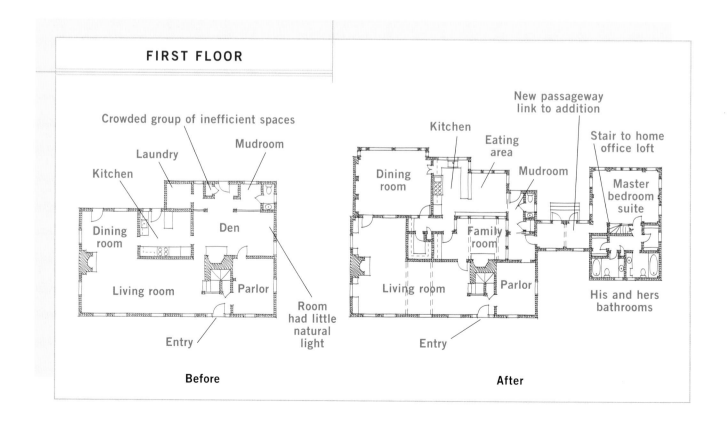

FIRST FLOOR

Before

Crowded group of inefficient spaces
Laundry
Mudroom
Kitchen
Dining room
Den
Living room
Parlor
Entry
Room had little natural light

After

New passageway link to addition
Kitchen
Eating area
Mudroom
Stair to home office loft
Dining room
Master bedroom suite
Family room
Living room
Parlor
His and hers bathrooms
Entry

The master bedroom soars a full story-and-a-half in height. The effect is open and airy, and yet the structural frame lends scale and maintains the historical context.

Georgian Colonial Hallmarks

AS THE COLONISTS BECAME more prosperous, many were eager to flaunt their new-found wealth with larger and more elaborate houses than the dimly lit, low-ceilinged Colonial dwellings of the previous generations. These fashionable houses, known as Georgian Colonials, were influenced by an interest in the Italian Renaissance movement that had already swept through Europe.

The style is characterized by a classical treatment of the facade, with decorative cornices below the eaves and elaborate details surrounding the entry door. High-style examples might have *quoins* — decorative blocks at the corners of the house. The front door was now finely crafted with a solid frame and raised panels. Classical details, such as pilasters and pediments over window openings, rounded out the kit of parts that architects and master craftsmen drew on to embellish the new houses.

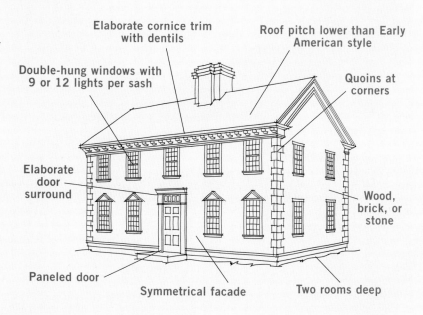

Elaborate cornice trim with dentils

Double-hung windows with 9 or 12 lights per sash

Roof pitch lower than Early American style

Quoins at corners

Elaborate door surround

Wood, brick, or stone

Paneled door

Symmetrical facade

Two rooms deep

The familiar symmetry of the Colonial facade was firmly established by this time, and the plan had evolved to a spacious two rooms deep. The rooms became taller—new prosperity meant a gentleman could now afford to *buy* firewood to heat a large house. And generously sized double-hung windows, with a sliding sash of 9 or 12 lights each, superseded the swinging casement.

The roof types of Georgian Colonials were varied, relying less on regional practice than on the preferences of the new owner. The Dutch gambrel was very popular, and it offered the practicality of a roomier attic. The hip roof of the southern French style crept northward through Virginia, and the simple gable of the northern colonies slid southward, sometimes appearing with a cross gable directly aligned with the entry below.

LEFT, **Viewed from across** pond and pasture, the addition appears as though it had been constructed 200 years earlier.

BELOW, **To make new space** for the dining room, a spot next to the kitchen was extended outward and roofed over. A small projection containing a sliver of a window cleverly articulates the potentially boxy form.

wall from the addition, creating what architects call a floating or detached *plane*. Although modern in concept, this detail corresponds nicely with the New England character of the house by adding yet another part to the traditional assemblage of additions and outbuildings. From inside the dining room, these narrow strips of glazing provide an unexpected source of light, making the new space all the more stimulating.

The home may seem to be made up of a hundred small parts, but both architectural history and good architectural practice ensure that everything comes together in a pleasing composition.

A Gourmet's Domain

ABOVE, **When contemplating a renovation,** consider changing the roles of rooms that no one seems drawn to. This new kitchen was constructed in a playroom that saw little use.

FACING PAGE, **A pot full of drama** is created by surrounding the cooking area with a bank of windows. A deep corner shelf holds a plant or two and is a handy spot to place spices and oil when preparing a meal. The low counter to the left is for rolling dough.

J OANNE AND NICK HAD MORE SPACE in their 1980s Colonial than they realized. When they approached their architect seeking advise on how to enlarge a cramped kitchen, he began by evaluating the floor plan with a fresh perspective. Rather than pursue the obvious direction of building an addition, they worked with a room in the home that was both underused and positioned just right for a kitchen.

A BLEND OF NEW IDEAS

The underused room, measuring nearly 28 ft. by 18 ft., had access to their spacious backyard and in-ground pool. The family had tried filling the room with the children's toys but the children rarely played there, opting to join their parents in the family room instead. And since any clutter could be seen from the formal entry hall by looking around the stair, it really wasn't suitable as a playroom. But the room would make a fabulous gourmet kitchen, and in the process, the current kitchen could be transformed into a new laundry room with enough space remaining for a new study for Nick.

For the sake of convenience, kitchens require a good link to where the cars are parked. Since this home's garage was below the main floor, the central staircase in

The focal point of this kitchen corresponds to the corner windows, setting up an interesting diagonal orientation to the plan. The seating side of the island is wrapped with a bar-height counter that blocks the view of dishes in the sink.

the large entry hall would have to be altered to include a flight going down to the lower level. That required removing the closet that had been under the stair—a small sacrifice to ease the chore of hauling in the groceries. The architect also specified the removal of the sidewalls beneath the stair, because they had obstructed the view between the family room and the dining room on opposite sides of the center hall. The stair is now supported by a group of slender posts, with an attractive wood baluster installed between them.

The lower walls of the entry hall stair were removed to improve sight lines to other areas of the home.

A Recipe For Work and Play

Today's kitchens often contain both a counter seating area and space for a kitchen table. Children or friends can hang around the counter and chat or do homework

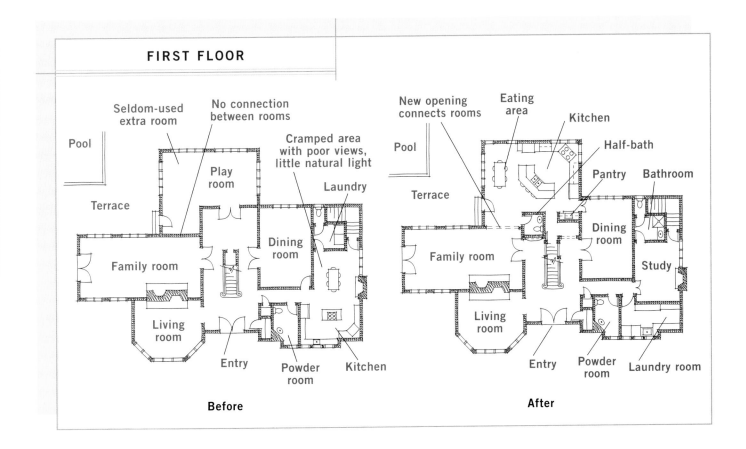

FIRST FLOOR

Pool

Terrace

Seldom-used extra room

No connection between rooms

Cramped area with poor views, little natural light

Play room

Laundry

Family room

Dining room

Living room

Entry

Powder room

Kitchen

Before

Pool

Terrace

New opening connects rooms

Eating area

Kitchen

Half-bath

Pantry

Bathroom

Family room

Dining room

Study

Living room

Entry

Powder room

Laundry room

After

One Step beyond Kitchen Fundamentals

VARIATIONS ☆

YOU'VE PROBABLY HEARD about planning work areas in a new kitchen in the form of a triangle. The objective is to place the three major components—sink, range, and refrigerator—within a few steps of one another for maximum efficiency. A plan following this common strategy will function reliably well. However, if you would like your kitchen to function *amazingly* well, try adding this to the formula:

★ Make your triangle a square, adding a suitably sized counter area as a fourth component—a place to make a sandwich, chop the veggies, and debone the snapper.

★ Position the refrigerator closest to the family room when establishing your four-corner layout; someone seeking a cold drink will be less likely to cross into the work zone while you're preparing a meal.

★ Add a second chopping area or prep station with its own small sink, outside the primary work zone to allow friends or children to help out. If space allows, design this area in such a way that access to the refrigerator can be had without crossing through the primary zone.

★ Create a place along the boundary of the work zone where children or friends can socialize with you while you work. This can be as simple as a counter or island with good lighting and comfortable seating.

Views to outside from sink area

Area for homework or socializing doesn't cross into work zone

To deck

To mud-room/ garage

To family room

2. Refrigerator

1. Sink

4. Range

Pantry

3. Work counter

To dining room

while you prepare a meal, and the nearby table can be set for a group or can hold a larger project. Joanne's new kitchen follows this model. A new island contains the sink, allowing her to face toward the table while chopping vegetables or cleaning up. On the other side of the table is a French door that provides her with a view outside as well. The back of the island is a full bar height of 42 in.—6 in. taller than normal, which conceals the sink area from those seated at the table.

Commercial ranges can be made an interesting focal point in a new kitchen—but not at the expense of convenience. A kitchen is a heavy work area and must function well to be considered successful. Joanne's cooking area, with a stainless-steel range, is positioned

to the other side of the island and catercorner to a bank of windows. A gleaming ventilation hood hangs above, floating free of the glass. The diagonal placement is an unexpected twist in the rectangular room and corresponds with the C shape of the generous island.

A few steps from the range, a lowered counter area was incorporated into the design to serve a double-duty function. This section of countertop is Joanne's baking area (see the photo on p. 79). It's positioned 4 in. lower, at 32 in., for working with dough. By lowering the counter slightly, you can position yourself over the work area and transfer your body weight to the rolling pin more effectively. Also, the lower work surface is at

the right height for the children to help in the kitchen without the need for a tippy foot stool.

BORROWING SPACE FROM ABOVE

The new kitchen doesn't have a second floor above. The room originally had been constructed on to the back of the Colonial as a separate appendage—similar to a screened porch. The design takes advantage of the overhead space that was concealed in the low attic by raising the ceiling up to the rafters. A tray shape was created by angling the sides of this recess inward, and a new skylight was installed to place natural light directly in the center of the room. The ceiling tray is also the source for the overhead artificial lighting, so the source of light remains consistent during daylight hours and after dark. For a finishing touch, the ceiling tray is adorned with an inlay of painted wood strips, attached to the drywall to create a decorative grid.

Because the existing space of Joanne and Nick's house was given a good, critical look, they were spared unnecessary construction costs—and a home that would have been too large. You may also benefit by considering if each room under your roof is used (and enjoyed) as much as it should be. It's an approach that can cut the fat from an overweight floor plan and introduce a banquet of fresh space at a bargain price.

CHAPTER THREE

RENOVATING A COLONIAL HOME

ABOVE, **A modern kitchen** nestles agreeably within a renovated home, thanks to the attention to detail: Cabinets with inset doors lend a traditional appearance, an authentic divided-light window recalls others throughout the home, and the timber structure responds to the era of the original house.

FACING PAGE, **A renovation project** can transform the ubiquitous postwar Colonial from tired to timeless. Here, window replacement, new exterior trim, and modifications to the the roof contributed to a proudly vertical stance typical of earlier Colonials.

THROUGHOUT THE COUNTRY, you can find a stock of older Colonials that are ripe for renovation. The oldest date back to the 1600s and 1700s and await an appreciative owner who can refurbish a slumping structural frame, replace weather-beaten siding, perform masonry repairs, and refinish wide-plank flooring. At the other end of the spectrum are the homes from the 1950s, 1960s, and 1970s that are showing their age and have outlasted homebuilding fashion—with old tile, pink plumbing fixtures, and avocado appliances that have somehow managed to escape earlier updates. The homes between these two extremes probably require attention to all of the above, along with the undoing of any poorly planned alterations constructed over the years. A spirited renovation can clean up these trouble spots and prepare your Colonial for raising your family in a fresh atmosphere without razing the house.

The side walls of the common postwar Colonial are often neglected. The absence of windows unnecessarily closes off light and views.

UPDATING A TIRED COLONIAL

Colonials of different vintages each present their own renovation challenges. Early American Colonials will likely have structural issues to uncover, and the new fixtures and products selected for the renovation will have to have some logical relationship to the heritage of the home. Later Colonials of the 1800–1900s will require attention to the abundant woodwork that was applied to the home, and you may find yourself sorting between the differing styles to learn which set of architectural rules to apply. The architecturally chal-

Adam Colonial Hallmarks

IRONICALLY, AMERICA CONTINUED TO LOOK to England for direction in art and style even after political control by the English had been overcome. The influence of the popular London designer Robert Adam could be seen in subtle changes to the two-story rectangular Colonial with its rigidly symmetrical facade.

The thick Georgian cornices and other architectural trimmings were reduced in favor of a delicate palette of classical details. New motifs were popularized, such as the urn and garland, inspired by the archaeological discoveries of Roman houses in Pompeii and Herculaneaum. The urn influenced window shapes and even oval-shaped entrance halls with graciously curving staircases. Over the front door, the use of an arched transom and a central Palladian window on the second floor had become a hallmark of the style. Windows became even taller and larger than in the Georgian style, and

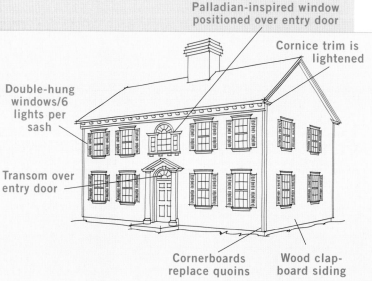

Palladian-inspired window positioned over entry door

Cornice trim is lightened

Double-hung windows/6 lights per sash

Transom over entry door

Cornerboards replace quoins

Wood clapboard siding

muntin patterns were reduced to six lights per sash. Adam-style houses were more likely to be expanded by projecting distinct wings from the sides.

The Adam style, representing a new era of democracy, was intended as a design attainable by every American. A wide range of examples remaining today can be found as high-style brick mansions in eastern cities and clapboard dwellings in the countryside.

lenged postwar Colonial might need an entire facelift to bring out a new personality. Regardless of the era, style, or type, the basic planning of the typical two-room-deep floor plan will need to be scrutinized to ensure that the renovated home will suit your family's lifestyle.

The battle of the bland

Speculative postwar Colonials were quick to construct, often at the expense of handsome detailing and proud proportions. And they are stingy when it comes to window selection and placement—there may be only one or two, if any, on the sidewalls, while the windows on the front of the house are frequently ganged together in pairs and are blocky in proportion. The normally steep roof pitch became shallow, and the combined effect

Renovation projects involve the spirited renewal of an existing house and often include the construction of a new addition. This renovated Colonial Revival, located in a small Maine town, has a gracious new portico at the entry, a large new wing to one side, and a refreshed overall appearance.

Double-Hung Heritage

☆ **THE DOUBLE-HUNG WINDOW** is the most common type used in the various Colonial styles. These windows were introduced in the early 1700s as a replacement for the original small, drafty casements—a window type that we often think of as contemporary, not Early American. Casements became impossible to close if the home settled or sagged even slightly over time, pushing the window frame out of alignment with the sash.

The dividing bars of a window are often referred to as *mullions,* but the correct term is *muntins* or

muntin bars. Muntins divide panes of glass, whereas mullions divide entire windows, as in a side-by-side grouping of two or more units.

casts a horizontal posture on the home. If the home is a *garrison* type, with an overhanging second floor, the horizontality is amplified even further.

You can counter this sleepy appearance by installing replacement windows that are positioned, and proportioned, like the Colonials from previous eras. In the 1970s Colonial shown on p. 85, individual windows with upright proportions replaced the originals, and to heighten the facade, a cross-gable was constructed on the low-pitched roof. The corners of the house were emphasized with wide pilasters to offset the horizontal step of the second-floor overhang.

Renovating a classic

Earlier Colonials, from the Georgians to the Revivals, come with their own special considerations. If the home predates about 1835, it was likely constructed with a heavy timber frame. As stout as the structure may seem, it will need to be scrutinized for water and insect damage, and defective structural members must be replaced. There are a number of specialty yards that stock reclaimed timbers from dismantled barns and

The two-story structure at the back of this home had to be demolished to make way for an addition that would better suit the needs of the owner, as well as better fit the appearance of the original house.

The renovation looks as though it was built some time ago, because it incorporates exterior details inspired by the original Colonial Revival.

ABOVE, **The staircase found** in the entry hall of nearly every Colonial can be made into a focal point. In this example, the job involved removing the walls beneath the stair to take advantage of shared views and light between the front and the rear of the home.

RIGHT, **To live in an Early American** home is to live with history. Reminders of how Colonists lived, worked, and socialized are evident in the architecture. The rustic yet cozy rooms and the squeaky floors are quirky to some, but many of us wouldn't want to live any other way.

houses for just such a project. In addition, you'll want to examine the condition of the siding and the abundant exterior wood trim carefully, looking for any signs of water damage, dry rot, or insect damage. If you're planning a renovation that will faithfully renew the original look of the home, don't rip off rotted boards until you, your architect, or the contractor has made a sketch to record the profiles and assembly of the old work so replacements can be fabricated.

Frequently, small additions or modifications constructed by earlier generations of the home's owners may have to be demolished to make way for a better home with a better functioning floor plan. The Colonial Revival shown on pp. 88 and 89, required the removal of a two-story extension before renovation work and the construction of a new, larger addition could begin. The new work pays closer attention to the original house by mimicking the complex trim details for an integrated appearance. And the architect was able to shape the new floor plan explicitly to the owner's needs, without being forced into a compromise brought on by someone else's pattern of living.

As one of your largest investments, a renovated house can be thought of as a financial concern that requires your careful attention. You'll want to inspect it annually and perform routine maintenance to keep it in prime condition.

Reviving Early American Colonials

Throughout the eastern United States, it's common to come across authentic Early American Colonial homes from the 1700s and even earlier. Homes of this era are small in scale, modest in plan, yet complex with character. Imagine coming home to a proud clapboard structure with an exposed timber frame, a massive stone chimney, cozy bedrooms, and planks of chestnut flooring 20 in. wide. Old homes such as these have fireplaces large enough to swallow a Volvo®, yet a six-foot visitor has to duck to pass through a doorway. They are a paradox of technological ingenuity and primitive shelter, of light-from-a-candle romance and reminders of the routine hardships faced by our ancestors. And they represent some of the most extraordinary homes in America.

After centuries of fending off storms, these homes will likely have surrendered to the destructive effects of water and the structure will have to be examined for deterioration, as mentioned above. To enable us to live comfortably yet retain the essential qualities of a historic dwelling, modern plumbing and wiring will have to be concealed within the exposed timber-frame structure. It's a difficult chore to route the waste pipes and supply lines carefully within the slim walls. Electrical wiring can be run beneath floors or in shallow channels cut into overhead beams.

Open house

In many Colonials, the lack of available floor space isn't really a problem. However, the way spaces are connected affects the usability of the home. The traditional, discrete rooms found in the typical Colonial can feel restricting, forcing certain activities into remote corners of the home. For example, it may be impossible to referee the children's card game while you pay the bills in another room. Your home should allow family life to be fluid,

A remodeling of the kitchen accompanies nearly all major renovation projects. In this example, a wall was removed to create an open connection between the table seating area and the kitchen work zone.

with visual communication between areas and versatile spaces that are suited to a variety of activities.

Reorganizing the floor plan during your renovation by altering a wall or two can improve this situation, allowing you to view through rooms instead of just down hallways. You may want to consider *removing* walls where a fully open connection between rooms is desired. Load-bearing walls can be altered or removed, but you'll need to engage a competent professional to specify exactly how this should be handled. In the home shown in the photo on p. 90 (top), the owners made the entry feel larger, while visually connecting the front and back of the house, by removing the walls below the main stair. The floor above is supported by concealed structural headers bearing on new posts, which are emphasized by special trim details.

Another benefit of opening walls between rooms comes when windows from one room share light with another, brightening the enlarged space. The typical two-room-deep Colonial floor plan is bound to have a dark corner somewhere, especially if there is an addition that buries a room in the middle of the floor plan.

WORKING WITH WHAT YOU'VE GOT

There seem to be two types of people who decide to renovate. One longs for the character of an old home but with a completely modernized interior and so seeks out a bargain-rate fixer-upper in an established neighborhood to create the ideal blend of old and new. The group has lived in his home for several years and is faced with catching up on much needed maintenance—in a home the family has likely outgrown. Such a family wants a new, larger house but has created bonding ties with the neighborhood and local schools. In both cases, an admirable side effect surfaces: One helps to keep community identities intact, and the other sets new standards for a neighborhood that has fallen into a depressed state.

Though you may have a lot of work ahead of you in terms of replacing windows, making repairs, replacing the roof, and painting, it's likely that the basic bones of

Beating the Weather

IT CAN BE UNNERVING (and very costly) to discover rotted woodwork during your renovation project. Before you remove soggy boards and give them the javelin heave into the Dumpster®, do a little architectural forensic work and determine why the damage occurred in the first place. Lack of adequate paint protection might be one reason, and that can be assuaged by stepping up the routine of annual maintenance. You should also examine the flashing, which is the metal strips used to prevent rain from entering the building through seams in the roof and walls. Even the joints created by slight projections, such as the casing around windows, must be protected. In any renovation project, check with your contractor to make sure all of the new work is properly flashed.

the house will make it another 100 years. This chapter shows several examples of how homeowners have accomplished the task of transforming an older, outdated Colonial into a bright, invigorating family environment that maintains the framework of Colonial style.

The Best of Both Worlds

ABOVE, **On the way** to the master bedroom, the owners pass beneath this dramatic cupola, centrally located over their own private hall.

FACING PAGE, **You can restrict** the renovation to only a particular zone of the house. This Colonial Revival from the 1930s received a considerable addition out the back, while the traditional rooms to the front were left intact. Alterations to the front facade involved no more than a fresh coat of paint.

CHIP AND DEBBIE, THE OWNERS of this Colonial Revival, lead a busy life. Both are highly involved in their children's activities, and like many of us, their professional lives are tugging at them constantly. They realized their suburban Connecticut home needed the kind of spaces where the family could gather and recharge. But they also enjoy entertaining and wanted to maintain a traditional dining room, living room, and center-hall entryway. The formal plan arrangement already provided by their classic Colonial home suited them just fine, and by creating new space designed for their informal family time, they could have the best of both worlds.

THE HEART OF THE HOME

The new kitchen and family room is the area of the house where Chip, Debbie, and the children can relax. These rooms are sized for multiple activities, and the height of the family room was determined by the wish to install an 11-ft. Christmas tree each December. The design corresponds with the typical Colonial pattern of using distinct rooms and acknowledges modern notions of liberated space with open planning for a sense of connectivity. From the kitchen, there are large passage-

The cabinets facing the table area are accessible from both sides, making setting the table or putting away dishes an easy chore. Pass-throughs and the glass doors admit daylight to the deep space, while allowing family members at the table to keep in contact with those working in the kitchen.

ways that allow communication, both verbal and visual, with the family room and the eating area to the sides. The openings in the kitchen partition also allow sunlight to penetrate through the deep room.

The cabinets between the kitchen and the eating area contribute to the flow of communication and light, and provide an element of convenience as well— there are operable glass doors on both sides, allowing the owners to put dishes away from one side and set the table from the other. The walls that define the kitchen have ample passageways to make it easy to get

to the table and navigate around work areas. Nearby, a back stair creates a shortcut between the kitchen and the second floor.

A GALLERY OF IDEAS

Instead of including a typical mudroom in the addition, a long gallery was developed that connects the new side and back doors. Although this space is utilitarian, it has been dressed up by using attractive yet rugged materials and by keeping the design simple and well ordered. The back of the family room fireplace is visible in the gallery, forming a natural stone backdrop for an old church pew. The family can enjoy the convenience of the pew, located just opposite a cubby storage area, to sit and slip on a pair of boots before catching the bus or playing in the Connecticut snow.

A bathroom with a seashore theme is positioned where it can be easily reached from the swimming pool without tracking water into other areas of the home. Wet feet were kept in mind when choosing the floor material for the gallery: Slate tiles, with a rough texture and just a hint of sea green color, were selected for their durability and beautifully natural appearance.

It seems you can never have enough storage space. With three young children—triplets in fact—Chip and

This mudroom extends the full width of the addition, offering accessibility to both the front courtyard and the pool area out back. Doors to the left lead to the cubby storage, the bathroom, and the garage.

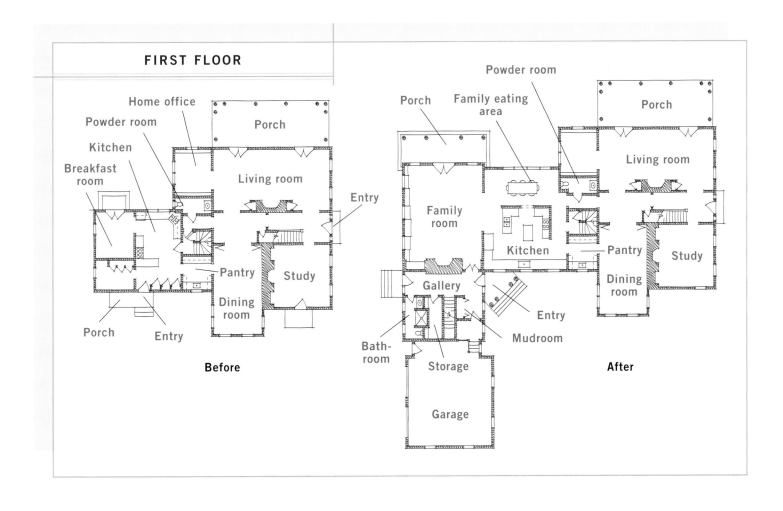

FIRST FLOOR

Before

Home office
Powder room
Kitchen
Breakfast room
Porch
Living room
Entry
Pantry
Study
Dining room
Porch
Entry

After

Powder room
Porch
Family eating area
Living room
Family room
Kitchen
Pantry
Study
Gallery
Dining room
Entry
Bathroom
Mudroom
Storage
Garage

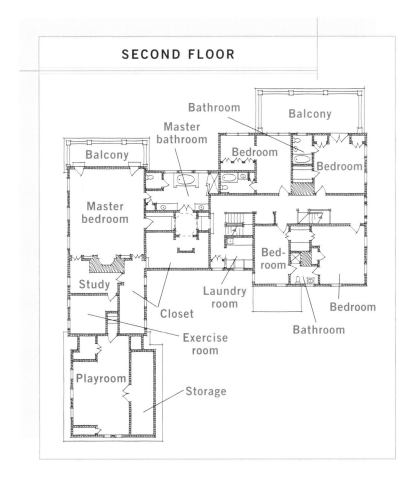

Balcony

Bathroom

Master
bathroom

Master
bedroom

Bedroom

Balcony

Bedroom

Study

Laundry
room

Bed-
room

Closet

Exercise
room

Bedroom

Bathroom

Playroom

Storage

Debbie knew this problem could catch up to them quickly if they didn't plan well ahead. The result is a compact, yet generously accommodating area with plenty of cabinets and cubbies for all the things the triplets could ever carry (see the photo on p. 101). The different types of storage are versatile enough to handle the children's needs as they grow, from book bags and lunch boxes to winter parkas and hockey sticks.

A private retreat

Directly above the new family room, but seemingly a world away, is Chip and Debbie's private retreat. This is their master suite, which is reached through a passage that is a treat of its own. The 11-ft. family room ceiling is just below the master suite, and a set of steps was needed to go up and over. The passage negotiates this change in level with steps that are grouped in twos,

Designed for stretching out and relaxing. The family room has abundant natural light, gives easy access to the terrace and pool, and is within a few steps of the kitchen.

Tall ceilings can sometimes leave us feeling cold, especially in a bedroom. But in this comfortable suite, the height is dampened by a pattern of woodwork on the ceiling and a deep band of molding at the ceiling line.

Colonial Siding

SIDING PROTECTS YOUR HOME'S structure from the weather—and its toughest adversary is water. If trim or siding traps or absorbs moisture because of an insufficient paint job or poor flashing, the wood can decay in a remarkably short period of time. Architects often specify siding products milled from western red cedar and eastern white cedar; both are naturally resistant to short-term moisture problems and to many damaging insects as well.

Siding plays a major role in the appearance of your home, and you'll want to evaluate the alternatives on the merits of their appearance and durability.

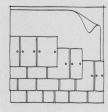

Sawn shingles. Often associated with houses along the East Coast, shingles are also found on the walls of inland Colonials. Some early houses were clad entirely in shingles except for the prominent front facade, which exhibited relatively more expensive clapboard.

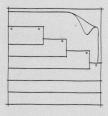

Clapboard or beveled siding. Clapboard with a simple profile was commonly used in Colonial architecture. It has a more refined appearance than a shingle wall. Cedar clapboard is smooth on one side and rough-sawn on the other, so you have a choice of finish.

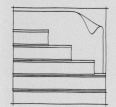

Decorative siding. Specific regions and towns favored certain types of decorative siding with a variety of profiles, such as beaded, channel, and shiplap. In Newport, Rhode Island, for example, many houses were clad in beaded siding.

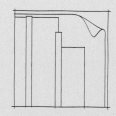

Board and batten. Board and batten siding was originally used for barns and outbuildings, but it since has been applied to new houses and additions as well, particularly when the architect wants to introduce a strong graphic image or suggest a less formal, rural effect. The boards are installed vertically, one next to the other, and the narrow battens are placed over the joints to keep out moisture.

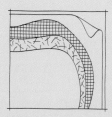

Stucco. Stucco is a cementitious material that is troweled over wire lath. Depending on the desired appearance and the artistic hand of the installer, stucco textures can vary dramatically, from glossy smooth to rough and rustic. While stucco is most often found in the South and Southwest, it also is used for more regal examples of Colonial architecture throughout the United States.

Brick and stone. Brick siding is second only to clapboard in its use for Colonials, and it is *the* material of the South, offering excellent weather protection and longevity. To help new work appear as if it had been done years ago, you can use "new-used" brick, which replicates weather-worn material. Stone creates a substantial, rustic, instantly old appearance, and it shares the excellent weather protection and longevity of brick.

LEFT, **A narrow space** off the mudroom is the perfect spot for an array of storage—from hooks to cubbies to cabinets.

BELOW, **A full tub offers** the promise of a rejuvenating soak in the master bath. The lower sashes of the windows are glazed with a textured glass to admit light while creating privacy from a nearby yard.

creating an elegant arrival to a luxurious space. A tall tower further reinforces the drama of the passage, spilling a copious amount of light where a second hall intersects. This crossaxis connects the walk-in closets to the master bathroom. A small but striking window, salvaged from the demolished portion of the house, was repaired and installed over the bathroom doors to capture light streaming down from the cupola (see photo on p. 94).

The bedroom is lofty but doesn't feel empty or out of scale. In fact, it seems cozy despite having a ceiling height of over 14 ft. The trick is in the trim detail, which was borrowed from the great mansions of Newport, Rhode Island. The room's height is tamed by the use of a large crown molding at the ceiling line, and a second decorative band positioned well below that. The **tray ceiling** is embellished with a contrasting decorative basket-like grid, which anchors the location of the ceiling and prevents it from vanishing above you. The woodwork looks elaborate but is really just painted 1x6 pine applied directly to the drywall. During construction, Chip joked of having "molding migraines" since the expense for such details can run pretty high. But without scale devices like these, you can end up feeling as though you were living in a drafty, echoing hall.

tray ceiling — A decorative raised area of a ceiling with equally sloping sides.

About-Face

ABOVE, **A study in contrast.** Traditional details on the original structure, such as the copper roof on the bay and special trim over windows, were added to emphasize the contrast between the old and the new.

FACING PAGE, **A grand hall,** also serving as a comfortable living room, links the twin structures that form the main house. The chic interior belies the modern surprises waiting just outside.

W HEN RENOVATING A TRADITIONAL RESIDENCE, architects often choose a harmonious design that blends with the existing structure. This strategy, when done well, can make it a challenging game to detect where the old house leaves off and the new begins. A second design approach is to create a deliberate distinction between an older house and a new addition by using similar forms and materials, though arranged in fresh ways. The new architecture relates to the old, but veers enough to be easily identified from the earlier periods of construction.

That being said, prepare to take an about face—a third strategy was applied in this remarkable renovation. Matthew and Jan's suburban Connecticut home unapologetically emphasizes the bold contrast between cutting-edge design and their traditional suburban Colonial.

A Project in Four Phases

Matthew and Jan's house doesn't necessarily fit the conventional definition of a Colonial. Not just because of four distinct modern additions constructed in phases over the past several years, but largely because of the original sprawling floor plan laid out in an unusual H formation. The form of the house is composed of twin two-story structures connected in the middle by a large

The first of four nontraditional additions was the home's back entrance and a work room used as a floral studio. The cutting garden is conveniently nearby.

hall. Each flanking structure compares in size and proportion to a modest Colonial home on its own, resulting in an impressive formal appearance.

When the owners began working with their architect to develop the first of four additions, they focused on an area of the house close to an adjoining garden, where they hoped to create a new mudroom. The new space was to hold the back door and have lots of storage and a laundry area nearby. The addition was also to contain a work area where Jan could create large floral arrangements. The architect quickly dropped the name mudroom for the more eloquent "flower room," and the utilitarian image of a mudroom was set aside as well, in favor of a space that promised to delight the senses as much as Jan's artistic floral arrangements.

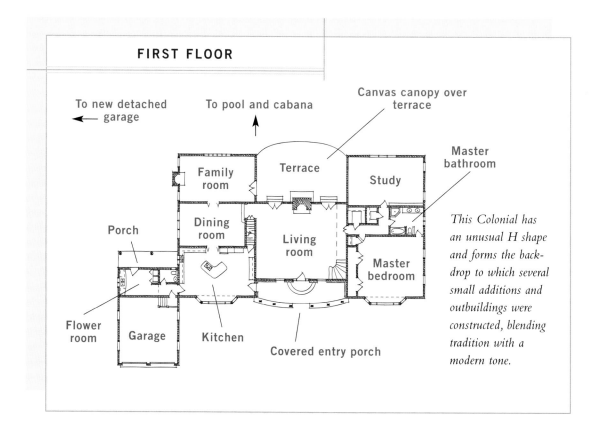

FIRST FLOOR

To new detached garage ←

To pool and cabana ↑

Canvas canopy over terrace

Family room

Terrace

Study

Master bathroom

Porch

Dining room

Living room

This Colonial has an unusual H shape and forms the backdrop to which several small additions and outbuildings were constructed, blending tradition with a modern tone.

Master bedroom

Flower room

Garage

Kitchen

Covered entry porch

The roof structure of the living room is echoed in the roof of the new porch, which precedes the grand space. The arc of the low stone wall matches the convex arc of the tilted wood beam precisely, preventing the accumulation of snow and ice in winter.

Several early attempts at creating a traditional addition that related to the existing house were deadends that left everyone frustrated. Then, during a design meeting the architect feared would be his last, the owners flipped through a book featuring the work of architectural Modernists. They couldn't help but comment excitedly at every turn of the page. Charming shingles and shutters didn't do a thing for Matthew and Jan. The stark drama of glass, stone, and steel were the couple's vice. A week later, the design for the new flower room had been approved and no one has ever looked back.

Following the success of the flower room, three additional projects were designed by their architect and one by the owners themselves. At the main entrance, a new canopy was constructed to welcome visitors. To the east of the flower room, a new two-car garage was built. And a virtual oasis awaits Matthew and Jan in the rear-most portion of the yard next to the swimming pool, where a sophisticated cabana with an adjoining arbor was recently completed.

Conceptually, the house is seen as the gracious host to modern guests, and has undergone some cosmetic renovation of its own. But not with a modern pencil in

hand. Changes to the original structure involved making sure the traditional details remained intact, in character, and in good condition to create a distinct emphasis between the old and the new.

A WELCOMING CANOPY

When you arrive at Matthew and Jan's home, a large, arcing canopy spanning between the twin Colonial wings promises shelter and a gracious welcome. The canopy also helps deflect the buildup of ice and snow near the doorway. The statement made by the entry roof is bold yet elegant. There are no classical details, and no single element competes for your attention. The entry reads as a unified whole, despite its many individual parts and pieces.

Once underneath, it's easier to appreciate the combination of materials that create this remarkable effect. Simple lumber rafters span in a poetic pattern overhead, following the arc of the supporting beam. Stone veneer

The cabana sits beneath an arbor constructed of rough-sawn cedar timbers. The cedar was brushed with a clear finish coating after it was allowed to weather to a silvery tone.

FACING PAGE, **The interior of the floral studio** is ruggedly striking, thanks to such materials as copper and natural slate. This addition also holds the home's laundry center and mudroom.

RIGHT, **The porch roof** arcs gracefully over this warmly illuminated entryway. This home has effectively married modern additions with the original traditional design.

ABOVE, **The arbor defines** the rear edge of the pool area, creating a shaded spot for outdoor dining without cutting off the view to the rest of the property. Viewed from the house, the arbor is relatively transparent and doesn't stand in the way of the natural surroundings.

RIGHT, **The owner developed** this practical and striking canopy for the sun-drenched rear terrace. Shade is created by the tug of a halyard to activate a system of stainless-steel cables, boat hardware, and canvas panels.

crisply defines the facade below the canopy, and black metal lighting sconces cast a warm glow throughout the space. The structural support for the canopy roof is a single 40-ft., curved, **laminated beam** supported by steel and wood columns. The beam is tilted forward, which sets up a subtle arc to the plan as well. The new stone base for the front terrace bows outward, following the curve of the canopy edge precisely (see the photo on p. 105).

A BACKYARD OASIS

The south-facing patio that occupies the backyard side of the H can get a little too much sun, starting around noon; so Matthew designed and built a unique shade canopy. It's constructed with a sailboat-like rigging system connected to canvas panels that can be unfurled by the tug of a halyard. When fully extended, the panels hang in long, billowy half cylinders creating a casual, Mediterranean atmosphere across the spacious terrace.

The most recent project Matthew and Jan completed was a new pool cabana with a rustic arbor built alongside. The cabana and arbor form a strong backdrop for the pool and help to provide visual definition for an otherwise ambiguous yard. The overhead structure of the arbor also offers a shady retreat for swimmers who wish momentarily to escape the direct sun.

These bold, contrasting design approaches never back down or stray indecisively and may not suit the average homeowner. Matthew and Jan chose roads less traveled, in search of an architecture expressive of their own unique character. Along the way, they discovered the beauty and simplicity exhibited in modern design—while all the while reinforcing their appreciation for traditional Colonial architecture.

The doors for the pool's changing cabana are of gray-toned, lead-coated copper and slide on concealed tracks. The remaining walls of the cabana are clad in conventional copper, except for the far sidewall and the roof, which are covered with translucent corrugated panels to admit light while retaining privacy.

laminated beam ⁀ A manufactured structural beam made from several layers of lumber glued together.

Heritage Reclaimed

Built in 1694, the house today appears as it may have 300 years ago. The double-hung windows probably would have replaced casements early on, perhaps in the first decades of the 1700s when hung sashes became popular.

W ALK THROUGH THE DOOR of this authentic Early American saltbox and you immediately sense you've entered a very special Colonial. The ceilings are low, the fireplaces are enormous, the wood is dark and rich, and the wide-plank floor squeaks a welcoming medley beneath your feet. I couldn't believe it when the owners told me the original construction date of the house was thought to be around 1694.

Frederick and Sandra, together with some very talented craftsman, have completely reconstructed this Guilford, Connecticut, Colonial they now call home. And in doing so, they have reclaimed a small piece of architectural heritage that was nearly lost to neglect. The restoration of the old house was a tremendous undertaking. There had been a successive chain of remodeling updates over many years, including the installation of drywall over original wood paneling, the subdividing of rooms, and the replacement of plank doors with common paneled doors. Frederick and Sandra lost no time in stripping away anything that wasn't true to an earlier era and even found a remarkable surprise along the way.

This restored Early American home provides the perfect setting for a collection of American art and antiques. The owners spent years painstakingly restoring the home, performing much of the work themselves.

Where Does the Wiring Go?

IF YOU FIND YOURSELF renovating a timber-frame home, you may face electrical wiring challenges. It requires careful planning and execution to modernize a home with electrical outlets, phone and data outlets, switches, lights, and smoke detectors.

Wall-mounted outlets, switches, and wall sconces can be installed between structural posts where there is sufficient space to handle the depth of a standard electrical box. If a structural post blocks wiring between connecting boxes, you can run the wire beneath the floor and then back up again, or drill a small hole to pass the wire through the concealed portion of the post as you would with studs in ordinary frame construction.

Floor outlets can make wiring simpler by allowing you to hide the wiring beneath the flooring. Lighting fixtures installed on the ceiling of an open structure can be a little trickier. Visible wiring tends to clutter the look of a historically pristine interior. One alternative, involving advanced carpentry skills, is to use a *Dutchman*, cutting a narrow channel for the wire in a beam and then concealing the work with a matching strip of wood. Another method, requiring less finesse, is to remove a floorboard from above the beam and cut a channel for the wire in the beam's top surface. Drill a hole where the fixture is to be mounted and lead the wire down into the room below. A flat "pancake" electrical box can be mounted onto the beam or, with a little careful cutting, recessed into the beam to mount the fixture.

warming room — Either of the two major rooms on the first floor of a northern Early American home, which was warmed by the massive central fireplace.

LIVING WITH THE PAST

Narrow doorways flank either side of the central entry hall. To the left is a **warming room** now used as a living room. The massive stone fireplace that commands this room was once used for cooking and heating water. Inside the firebox there is an iron swing-arm to hold pots and a tiny alcove that was used as an oven (see the photo on p. 119).

During the restoration, the rustic timbers of the living room underwent a careful cleaning and inspection.

The kitchen connects with the family room and has easy access to the nearby dining room. A narrow back stair leads to the upper floor bedrooms and is just visible in the small peek-through above the kitchen counter. Despite its small size, this opening keeps the kitchen from seeming isolated by providing a glimpse into neighboring areas.

In a few areas, deteriorated structural members had to be replaced entirely. Replacements were hand selected from a supplier of reclaimed beams and lumber. The flooring underwent a similar scrutiny. Split boards were repaired by gluing and doweling, and an occasional worn-out board had to be replaced.

In the opposite room, currently used as the dining room, workers discovered the subtle use of decoration in the woodwork. The timber structural beams have a decorative chamfer cut along the exposed corners giving them a refined appearance. Looking closer, the faint markings of painted stenciling could be seen along the length of the beams. It's not an unusual decorative treatment for a house of this era, but stenciling seldom survives so many years without being painted over or stripped away.

The dining room fireplace, though quite large by today's standards, was probably used for heating only, because cooking took place in the other room. Also referred to as the *best* room, the refinements in the dining room suggest it was likely used as a celebratory room for meetings, entertaining, and special meals (see the photo on the facing page).

The new kitchen makes no attempt to fit in with the 1600s home it serves. The design is deliberately contemporary to distance itself from the restored structure.

An early addition

Behind the living and dining rooms is a space that runs the length of the house. Today, the owners use this area as a family room, but 300 years ago this was the summer kitchen. The largest fireplace in the house is in the center of this room, which was once an open-air cooking area. You might say these were the very first home additions, since the summer kitchen was often covered with a roof for shade and rain protection and later closed in for added interior space—creating what we know as the saltbox.

The modern kitchen that services the house today is in a discreet addition off the back corner of the family room (see photo on facing page). Frederick and Sandra,

A second bedroom has just enough ceiling height to sqeak in a four-post bed.

After having been neglected for many years, this Early American home was brought to perfect condition by its new owners during a carefully executed reconstruction.

Chamber

Kitchen

Buttery (or pantry)

Cupboard

Warming room (or hall)

Best room (or parlor)

Entry

Massive central chimney

Before (shown as it likely appeared in the 1700s)

Pantry/laundry

Kitchen

Bath-room

Great room

Cupboard

Living room

Dining room

Guest bedroom

Entry

After

ABOVE, **A primitive plaster finish** enlivens the walls of an upstairs bedroom. The locations of the former casement windows are marked by wood planks on the wall, which are removable for purposes of historic analysis.

FACING PAGE, **The medieval plaster design** was scratched in freehand, and it displays a charming, improvised quality that is a world away from printed wallpapers.

recently schooled in the theories of architectural restoration, decided to create a kitchen that was not an Early American look-alike. The kitchen addition uses glass sliding doors for lots of sunlight, a durable slate floor, modern appliances, and granite work tops. The design allows for efficient performance—and its own demise. The owners explain that if the house were ever to undergo a preservation in the strictest sense, the new kitchen could be demolished with only minor repair work required to restore the original structure.

Upstairs, the roof extension of the saltbox is just tall enough to stand in. The owners took advantage of this area to create a new hallway, accessed by a narrow back

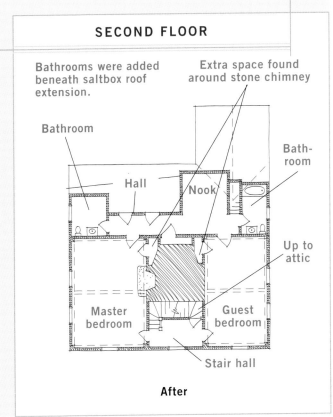

SECOND FLOOR

Bathrooms were added beneath saltbox roof extension.

Extra space found around stone chimney

Bathroom

Bath-room

Hall

Nook

Up to attic

Master bedroom

Guest bedroom

Stair hall

After

stair from the family room below. The hallway conveniently links the bedrooms and harbors a thoroughly modern convenience—a bathroom. Frederick and Sandra's saltbox is an original—on the bathroom wall, you can see the clapboard siding that was in place before the summer kitchen was roofed over (see the top right photo on p. 118). The owners decided to leave the old siding as a decorative finish as well as a record of the home's evolution.

A remarkable discovery

While stripping wallpaper from the upstairs guest bedroom, the owners uncovered an unusual and striking plaster finish called *pargeting*, a popular decorative treatment found in English homes of the 1600s by which a wood tool was used to scribe fanciful patterns in wet

RIGHT, **Weathered clapboard,** found fully intact in the attic of the roof extension, was left in place for a rustic effect in the new bathroom. The clapboard serves as a reminder of the home's evolution as it passed from one owner to the next. Beyond the plank door, electric wall sconces cast a warm glow in an otherwise shadowy hall.

plaster. According to author and history scholar Abbott Lowell Cummings, this is the only example of pargeting known to exist in the United States. The owners carefully cleaned the plaster and, after consulting with preservationists, sealed it with a single coat of water-based paint to fend off the wear of daily life (see the photos on pp. 116 and 117). They chose a color close to the original and even left a large patch unpainted to aid in future preservation efforts.

Frederick and Sandra have dovetailed the architectural and cultural legacy of their Colonial with their need for a comfortable, livable home. And they've been able respectfully to incorporate this history with their everyday lives. Their antique home stands as a tribute to the past and to the success of their remarkable efforts.

LEFT, **The fireplace in the summer kitchen** now displays a collection of cooking tools from the 1700s. The ancient chimney flues were professionally lined with mortar during the restoration, making the original fireplaces fully functional (and safe) for at least another century.

The original stone fireplace dominates the first floor warming room. The owners use the fireplace to display Early American artifacts related to everyday life of an era long past. To the right is a cupboard that displays early china and pottery. The cupboard is protected by the property deed—the vintage documents dictate that the cupboard cannot be modified or removed.

Two
If by Sea

The blue waters of Long Island Sound are just steps beyond the soft tone of the porch deck of pau lope, a tropical hardwood. Much harder and more durable than cedar or pressure-treated decking, this wood has recently come into favor. The tough surface weathers to a pleasing silvery tone and requires little or no maintenance.

W HEN KEEN AND SALLY SET ABOUT REBUILDING a family home on the Connecticut shore, they called on architect Tony Terry for advice. Built by Sally's grandfather in the 1900s, the home was in need of a major renovation. Tony analyzed the floor plan and explained that the old home "suffered from strained internal relationships," brought on by a century of hasty additions and oddly partitioned rooms. Furthermore, the house was worn out: The bathroom fixtures were stained, the mechanical equipment was coughing, the roof was no longer a match for New England nor'easters, and the drafty windows let in much more than just the views of Long Island Sound. Keen and Sally wanted to start fresh and develop new rooms, carefully arranged to share with extended family during summer.

The architect took the couple's wish list to his office and designed a double Colonial: a "front house" with views to the Sound and excellent sun exposure and a "back house" that looks out on a small cove and quiet marshlands. The completed design maintains the appearance of the original house. And Sally, who had spent many summers in her grandfather's house, appreciated the family memories conjured up by Terry's nostalgic shaping of the "new" forms.

An angled bay projects from the side of the back portion of the house, allowing a view past the front section. The deep overhang of the bay mimics the adjacent roof, elongating the effect of the wrap-around porch.

The open porches face the water while shading the house from the sun. The new house takes its cues from the original. The architect chose to retain certain elements of the outdated home, such as the open porches and the distinctive curving roof line, while providing an updated, open floor plan for a modern lifestyle.

FAMILY PLANNING

The south side of the house is nearly identical to the original, but the plan reveals how many changes actually took place. The former layout was restrictive, while the new plan has open spaces and wide views. Tony developed a new living room with a wall of windows and a French door directed toward Long Island Sound. A deep wrap-around porch protects the room from a possible overabundance of direct sun and has become the setting for lazy afternoons spent enjoying the shore from the seat of a teak rocker. A small study is tucked in along the east side of the home, next to the living room. Though private, the study also enjoys views to the Sound and access to the gracious porch.

A new kitchen, sitting area, and dining area are located within a single long room in the rear portion of the double Colonial. At one end, the dining table nes-

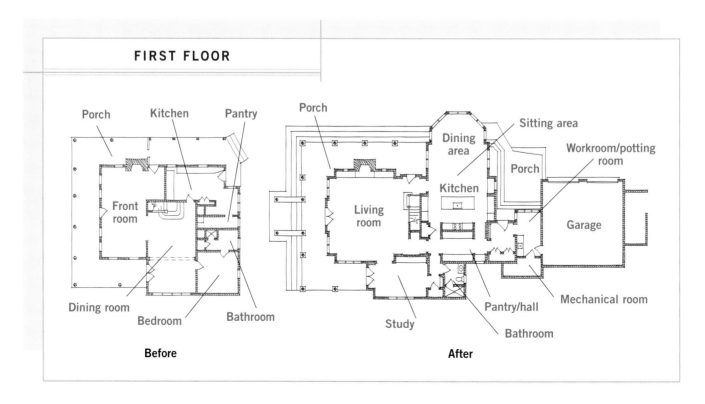

FIRST FLOOR

Before: Porch, Kitchen, Pantry, Front room, Dining room, Bedroom, Bathroom

After: Porch, Dining area, Sitting area, Workroom/potting room, Porch, Kitchen, Living room, Garage, Study, Pantry/hall, Bathroom, Mechanical room

Before

After

ABOVE, **The porches and balcony** are designed for outdoor living. The architect chose exterior materials characteristic of seaside architecture: white cedar shingles, lead-coated copper, and painted trim.

LEFT, **The architect maintained the** uniquely sweeping roof of this house, shown here before its extensive renovation.

RIGHT, **A glass door** opens to a shared ocean-front balcony from each of two guest rooms. The casement windows can open completely to catch prevailing breezes— a welcome option for an oceanfront home.

ABOVE, **Staircases can become** functional sculpture in any home. The architect designed the newel posts and decorative caps specifically for this project. Architects can bring much more to a project than basic planning. If your budget allows, think of requesting custom detailing right down to the cabinet knobs.

tles into an enormous angled bay, which extends beyond the living room to offer a panorama of the seaside landscape. At mealtime, Keen and Sally can enjoy 180 degrees of natural scenery, sweeping from the shore to marshlands and cove.

The kitchen is at the opposite end of the long room, separated from the dining area by a small seating group. By placing seating in this location, a buffer is created between the ritual of dining and the reality of a kitchen that's in open view. It's also a casual spot to hang out and chat with the cook before dinner. Tony sees this versatile room as the social nucleus of the home. And in fact, the dining table has become a favorite place for card games or simply sipping tea and watching the sea. The intimate seating area fosters close conversation, and the cook is never left alone behind a closed door.

Tony positioned the main entrance and stair hall where the two halves of the house meet. In plan, the entry makes for a healthy transition between the front and the back of the house by creating some separation between the large living room and the kitchen seating area. This separation also benefits the exterior. Without it, we wouldn't be able to enjoy the clarity of the two big gabled forms. And, practically speaking, if the roofs

A relatively compact kitchen shares space with a casual seating area. The introduction of an intimate seating near the kitchen has become a popular planning concept, allowing the cook to keep up with the conversation before mealtime.

Making a Case for Wood

YOU MAY FIND MANY ALTERNATIVES to wood siding, windows, and doors on the market. Vinyl and metal products tend to be durable and inexpensive, they clean easily, and they are often advertised as never needing to be painted. Nevertheless, I continue to recommend that homeowners stick with good old-fashioned wood, for a number of reasons.

Moisture control. Vinyl siding has weep holes to let out water that enters its seams, but it is installed over a type of insulation board that traps moisture, so the wood of the home is prone to decay and mildew. While vinyl may be maintenance free on the *outside,* there can be unseen damage taking place on the inside.

Insulation value. Metal-door manufacturers advertise the benefit of greater energy savings because their doors are insulated. But a metal door *has* to be insulated or it'll turn so cold in the winter that you'll stick to it! In contrast, wood is a natural insulator.

Color. A disadvantage of vinyl products that never need painting is that they won't do a good job of holding paint should you want to change the color. And using paints specifically designed for vinyl products defeats the purpose of never having to paint.

Authenticity. Unlike wood windows, vinyl windows do not come with the option of a true-divided-light sash. You have to settle for a snap-in grille instead of the real thing. Molded or stamped doors lack the crisply edged panels of wood doors. Although some manufacturers mold a wood grain onto their doors to make them appear more realistic, this doesn't make them look convincing— a high-quality wood door actually has a smooth surface.

were nearly touching, the construction detail required to shed rainwater from the converging slopes would be prone to leaks.

The entire second floor was designed for easy housing of visiting family members. There are four bedrooms in all, three of them oversize to make lengthier stays comfortable, and two of them opening out to a shared seaside deck. Keen and Sally's master bedroom suite is located on the third floor. Tucked beneath the twin gables, this suite offers a surprising amount of floor area for the owners' year-round retreat, including a spacious study with views toward the marsh.

BUILDING RELATIONSHIPS

The architect shaped this distinctive haven by using an **additive** technique. Behind the complex layers of columns, porches, dormers, bays, and projecting roofs lies a very basic shape—the familiar two-story Colonial. The new house is clearly different from the original, and yet neighbors who knew the old house often comment on the similarities. That's because Tony maintained many of the existing features, including the multiple porches, the distinctive curving roof (known throughout the neighborhood for a century), and the compact scale. The new structure acknowledges the strong influence provided by the surrounding homes and the sense of family history this special place holds for Sally and her siblings.

Formerly a warren of small spaces, the new living room opens to unobstructed views and easy access to the porch, lawn, and beach. Muntins are used sparingly in the windows to emphasize the view.

additive ⌐ Enclosed space that projects outward from a building, contributing to its form and appearance.

Rural Victory

The chinking between logs is composed of an insulating filler material sandwiched between a plasterlike acrylic-based coating. The weathertight chinking adheres to the logs yet remains elastic, allowing movement as the structure expands and contracts with changes in the weather.

H OMEOWNERS GWEN AND JIM DESCRIBE their rural Pennsylvania Colonial as "being equally inaccessible from everywhere." They came across the home, sited on a 16-acre plot of land, a decade ago and began collecting ideas on how to go about enlarging and renovating the 1741 stone structure, intending on paying respect to its early German origin. It was a puzzle that took years for Gwen to solve.

It wasn't until Gwen began working with architect Peter Zimmerman that the solution became clear. They would add a small addition to the rear of the home for informal dining with seating nearby. An existing stone appendage, ideally positioned to serve the dining area, would accommodate the kitchen and a new hall. The addition would not be of stone to match the house, but instead of rustic logs, a historically compatible means of construction. Peter explains there was no attempt to make a replica of the house. "The intent was to provide a livable building," he says, "sensitive to the historic nature of its site and its natural environment."

The renovated house and its new addition appear firmly anchored to the site, rather than looking as if it had been plopped down on the surrounding landscape.

ABOVE, **The living room contains** a smaller, refined fireplace in contrast to the large hearth in the entry hall. A second access to the new addition was created in this room, allowing a circular flow to the floor plan. The thickness of the exterior stone wall is evident in the deep door jamb of the passageway.

RIGHT, **The timber ceiling** frame is constructed with the same Old World methods used to support a second floor—a central summer beam supporting joists to either side. The open framework is set at about the same height as the ceilings in nearby rooms to ease the dramatic difference in volume between the addition and the house.

ROCK THE HOUSE

Despite the German heritage of this Pennsylvania Colonial, the floor plan of the original house follows the English pattern of northeastern construction quite closely. A large stone chimney dominates the center of the house, with fireboxes on both sides to warm the lower rooms. The rectangular form of this stone Colonial isn't graced with the typical balanced facade however. The door is well left of center, having originally been the entry to what was known as a *half house*—a small home built with the idea of expanding as soon as the means became available. The early owners must have found their American dream, and the house received a stone addition in the very late 1700s.

In the design of the latest renovation, Peter opened the plan as much as possible, doing away with partitions that were installed by earlier owners. The original floors

Winter visitors arriving by either sleigh or SUV are made welcome in the home's entry hall by the crackling warmth of this original stone fireplace, finished with white-washed plaster. The passage beyond was cut through the thick stone wall and leads to the new addition.

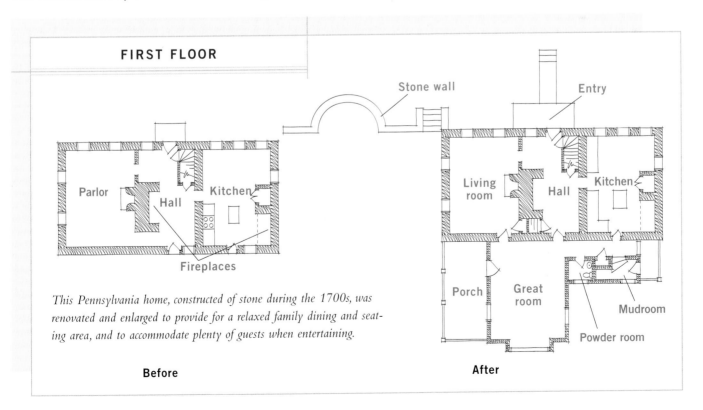

FIRST FLOOR

This Pennsylvania home, constructed of stone during the 1700s, was renovated and enlarged to provide for a relaxed family dining and seating area, and to accommodate plenty of guests when entertaining.

Before

After

Conservation and Wetlands

☆ **THAT RAIN GULLY** between you and your neighbor's house might not simply be a ditch for storm runoff. It could be part of a larger inland wetlands ecosystem. There are strict limitations on how close you can build to the edge of wet areas, and it pays to review the town maps even if an obvious brook, marsh, or pond is located on your property. In many cases, the boundary lines shown on a conservation map will be more restrictive than the visible portion of the wetlands feature on your site. Regulations also exist to prevent soil runoff from an open excavation into sensitive areas. Because of this erosion control, you may be required to install silt fencing or hay bales at the perimeter of your site. If you live in a coastal environment ask your conservation official for additional limitations that may apply to your property.

RIGHT, **The old exterior stone wall** remains visible in the new dining area and creates a romantic backdrop for an evening meal. The chandelier holds candles, not electric bulbs, to heighten the effect.

FACING PAGE, **The log-and-chink construction** creates a dramatically graphic interior finish for the new dining and sitting areas, reinforcing the rustic character of the original house. Daylight floods in from the box bay window at the end of the room and from two small dormers located above.

were refinished, and the stone walls of the fireplaces were repaired and whitewashed.

CABIN FERVOR

Although the addition is of a different material, it nestles in harmoniously with the house. Selected logs were hewn square and stacked, and the spaces between them were filled with plaster in a traditional process called *chinking*. The foundation for the addition, visible above the sloping grade, is a veneer of natural local fieldstone that matches the original house precisely. Even the new mortar that fills the gaps between the stones was tinted to match exactly the weathered mortar of the existing house.

The new room adjoins the back of the two-story stone structure and is accessed by two openings cut through the thick wall. One leads in from the living room, the other from a hall Gwen and Peter carved

from the kitchen wing. The ruggedly textured stone wall in the addition is left visible as a foil to the horizontal log construction. Gwen, an interior designer, furnished the new space with antiques and other furniture she had collected over many years, and she revels in the dramatic contrast between the natural materials and the polished Queen Anne table and chairs.

Centered over the table is a massive summer beam, typical of those used in timber construction. From the beam, Gwen has hung a blacksmith's iron chandelier that is fitted with candles instead of electric lights. The atmosphere created by the flickering glow of the candles casts deep shadows on the rugged materials and radiates an orange blush on the cathedral ceiling above,

taking Jim and Gwen's dinner guests back to the era when the stone house was first inhabited.

Opposite the dining area is a spacious seating group with a box bay window projecting from the cabin's wall. Gwen tiled the windowsill, creating a deep shelf for potted house plants. It's also a convenient place for extra seating when a large group fills the house during a party.

From the side of the room, a glass door leads to a summer porch, which faces a small pond on the property. The porch is deep enough for cushy seats and a small table to while away the evening hours comfortably in the quiet seclusion of this inaccessible full-time getaway.

Uncommon Place

The second-floor overhang found on many Colonials adds about a foot to the width of the plan on that level. Here, an interesting bracket is included, installed over paneled corner trim.

OUR HOMES TELL A GREAT DEAL ABOUT who we are. Simple or complex, daring or reserved, we express our values and personalities outwardly, through architecture, for all the world to see. When Scott and Mary Liz realized their 1970s Colonial home didn't express who they really were, they decided it was time for a much needed renovation—beginning with a facelift of their home's dated exterior. In addition, Mary Liz wanted an expanded kitchen with plenty of room for counter seating and a kitchen table. Scott, a professional engineer, wanted the informal dining space in the new kitchen to be lofty and expressive of the relationship between architecture and structural engineering, between art and technology. Both were after a comfortable family room with ready access to the backyard, and both thought the entryway felt cramped for a home of this size (almost 3,500 sq. ft.).

The couple began by enlisting the help of friend and architect Richard Hein to prepare drawings for the project, while Scott designed the structure. The team worked out an octagonal addition with a hidden steel frame for the new kitchen. Mary Liz led the direction for the face-lift, suggesting they first modify the roof

This spec Colonial was stripped bare and transformed to a home with a timeless appeal. New crossgables, siding, exterior trim, windows, and doors were composed with a traditional sensibility that blurs the date of the home's original construction.

The shape of the new roofline outside is reflected in a varied ceiling line inside, bringing a welcome spatial variety to an otherwise basic room.

lines of the Colonial to create visual interest. Richard designed a large central gable for the main house and smaller gables at the flanking ends.

FROM HOUSE TO HOME

Scott and Mary Liz's architect was more than competent at meeting their goals for the new addition and the roof modifications, but other commitments pulled him away from the project at a critical time. The couple turned to my architectural firm to complete the detailing that would make this house a home. Our approach to the exterior renovation involved the stripping of the entire exterior, right down to the sheathing. The windows and doors were discarded and the stingy, precast entry platform was demolished. We installed clapboard siding and painted wood casing for an unmistakable traditional look. The corners of the Colonial are empha-

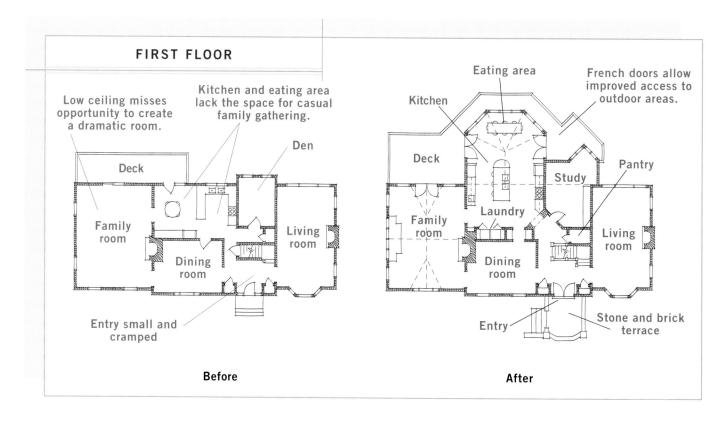

FIRST FLOOR

Before:
- Low ceiling misses opportunity to create a dramatic room.
- Kitchen and eating area lack the space for casual family gathering.
- Den
- Deck
- Family room
- Dining room
- Living room
- Entry small and cramped

After:
- Eating area
- French doors allow improved access to outdoor areas.
- Kitchen
- Deck
- Study
- Pantry
- Laundry
- Family room
- Dining room
- Living room
- Entry
- Stone and brick terrace

Before

After

The kitchen addition rises a story and a half and has the festive air of a gazebo or garden tent. Light pours in from the clerestory windows on all sides, helping make this an uplifting place to enjoy a great meal and take in the wide-open view of the yard. The countertop in the foreground is Bahia granite, a rare stone dappled in a distinctive blue.

Careful attention to the details was included in the design of the new built-in bookcases—right down to the miniature columns that frame an attractive arched niche.

center-matched siding ⌐
Interlocking wood boards, installed side-by-side, with a tight, barely visible joint.

sized with richly detailed pilasters and the second-floor overhang is finished with a wide, painted band supported by brackets at either end that evoke a turn-of-the-last-century feel. In the new gables, we used a smooth, painted surface made up of **center-matched siding** to contrast against the linear texture of the clapboards. The center gable has a large arch that corresponds with brand-new arched windows in the adjacent wing. The final touch was the installation of a circular window in the attic for visual interest.

PERSONAL APPOINTMENTS

The special care given to the exterior of the house carries through to the rooms within. Arriving in the foyer, guests now enjoy a preview of the rooms beyond, because the walls below the stair were removed to extend the space visually. The remaining structure required to support the top of the stair and the second-floor framing was clad in painted trim with a whimsical column detail borrowed from a local university library.

The renovated family room has become a more dynamic space created by the small gables Richard added. They translate to mini-cathedral ceilings, increasing the volume of the room and allowing the height necessary for the new arched transoms. A group of four arched windows were installed high in the end wall designated for bookcases and a cabinet for electronic gear. The custom built-in has a large shelf just below the level of the windowsills. The casing used throughout the room wouldn't hold a candle in relation to the depth of the cabinet and would cause the windows to appear flat. We installed a deep surround at the arched windows supported by mahogany brackets. A mahogany medallion is centered in the arch and echoes the circular window outside in the new gable.

ABOVE, **The family room** was enlarged by raising the ceiling to the underside of the rafters. The floor area is the same, but the room's dimensions feel much larger because of the increased volume. The ornate storage unit is the new focal point of the room and rises to encompass the group of arched windows in the end wall.

LEFT, **Hand-crafted hardwood brackets** and "tassels" support an extraordinarily deep window casing. The fine detail work combined with the extra depth of the window surround was necessary to remain in concert with the overall design.

☆ Classical Revival Hallmarks

THOMAS JEFFERSON IS CREDITED with the introduction of Classical architecture in America. The models of ancient Roman architecture and the work of Italian architect Andrea Palladio (1510–1580) influenced the design of his famous Virginia home, Monticello, and his architectural ideals were called on to create new government buildings that were to represent a young democracy called the United States.

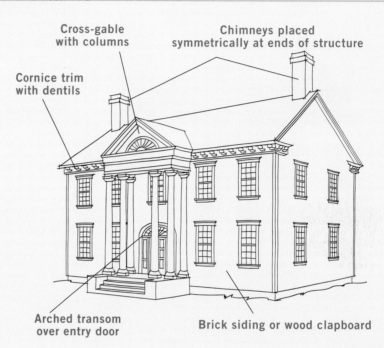

Cross-gable with columns

Chimneys placed symmetrically at ends of structure

Cornice trim with dentils

Arched transom over entry door

Brick siding or wood clapboard

Jefferson's home fueled an interest in classical design; by the 1790s, a new direction had been established, as the popular details and components found their way into homes throughout the settled portions of America. The rectangular, two-story Colonial became the canvas on which a new visage of styling was applied. The first classically styled houses appeared in the South and were often brick. Adorned with a cornice and dentils at the eaves, they had a relatively shallow roof pitch and a templelike crossgable with two-story-tall columns surrounding the customary symmetrical facade. Like the Adam houses, the central front door and the window directly above were emphasized with arched windows and transoms.

Jefferson's aspiration to copy the architecture and virtues of the much respected ancient Roman Republic eventually gave way to a rising interest in ancient Greek classicism. The familiar Colonial house and a pattern of planning that had been in use for over a century shifted momentarily to the Greek Revival style, which introduced a new plan layout accessed from the narrow side of the rectangular structure. The Colonial lay momentarily dormant until the style reemerged in the 1880s in a successive wave of revivals, including Neoclassicism, that continued virtually uninterrupted until World War II.

The family room is just a few steps away from the new kitchen, where the octagonal space for the dining table reaches high above the floor, stepping into a clerestory two-thirds of the way up (see the photo on p. 137). The faceted joints of the hip roof are enhanced with wood ribs, and the ceiling itself is finished with painted tongue-and-groove boards. The large space elicits a nearly festive feel, as though you were under the canopy of a massive tent. Aside from the wood ribs, there are no other visible structural ties or components because of the steel frame hidden within. Daylight floods into the kitchen from the large windows and the clerestory above. Although the kitchen is located to the

The front approach to this Connecticut Colonial includes a brick and stone patio gracious enough for a small table and chairs. The low stone wall, set at a standard seating height of 16 in., accommodates extra visitors.

interior of the large room, Mary Liz doesn't feel cut off from the view thanks to the expanse of glass.

In some ways, the renovated house appears contemporary, though it is undeniably traditional. It's fresh yet familiar, giving the rejuvenated structure a sense of enlivenment and an appropriate picture of the family who resides within.

CHAPTER FOUR

BUILDING A NEW COLONIAL HOME

Building new in the Colonial style doesn't mean making slavish copies of old houses. A passionate abstraction, this Colonial reinterpretation links the past and the resent with a sensibility suited to the individuality of the owners.

THE RENOVATED HOMES in the preceding chapters have shown how architects and homeowners have raised the bar for the Colonial. The blending of old and new concepts has transformed traditionally prim floor plans into versatile, open arrangements of spaces. And fresh interpretations of the exterior continue to draw on the past, sometimes quite subtly. This chapter offers innovative examples of how the Colonial bloodline can be adapted to reflect not only how we live but also how we potentially could live. Some of these homes are in step with the historic progression of the Colonial house type, while others skip a few evolutionary steps and are far from routine. Hopefully, you will be able to pick up invigorating ideas of how a new Colonial can shape your daily life.

STARTING FROM SCRATCH

Designing and building a new home is one of the largest and most challenging projects you may ever

Colonial houses have evolved significantly in planning and creative expression over many generations, but they still need to dwell comfortably within their surroundings. This new Maryland home perpetuates regional patterns and the architectural character of older, nearby homes.

encounter. But it's also one of life's great opportunities. Whether you're just starting out with a small dwelling, ramping up to something larger, or composing a dream getaway in a quiet locale, you'll find that a Colonial can be made to feel roomy, flexible, and stylish while indulging a spectrum of budgets and needs.

Many families choose a two-story Colonial for its stalwart solidity, the sense of security in the placement of bedrooms on the second floor, and a promise of comfort within the potentially ample footprint. Homeowners also may want to present a quiet or conservative image to the neighborhood, while not smothering their creative expression. Designing and constructing a new Colonial can satisfy all of these requests—there is flexibility behind that somewhat conventional facade. It is a home that can be added onto

logically and efficiently over time as needs change and families grow. New Colonials can follow historic models precisely, or be cleverly modified, depending on your family's sense of style. And as for the bottom line, the Colonial is a good investment, appealing to a wide demographic of home buyers.

Building a new Colonial can sometimes be more economical than renovating your older home or breathing new life into a fixer-upper, because adapting existing work often involves complex construction challenges. A new home gives you the chance to orient activities and spaces to suit the features and sunlight particular to your property—all while maintaining the Colonial's formal nature. Designing a new home also gives you the benefit of sizing and shaping spaces to your particular requirements. Renovation projects

RIGHT, **The gabled form** of these dormers takes the shape of little houses, hearkening back in an abstract way to the simple dwellings of long ago. The dormers bring light into the modern space in a more intriguing manner than the common rectangular skylight.

FACING PAGE, **The architectural details** of traditional styles are more costly to produce, install, and maintain than those of bare postwar Colonials. The payoff comes with the satisfaction of creating a home rich with historical associations.

style guide ☆

Colonial Revival Hallmarks

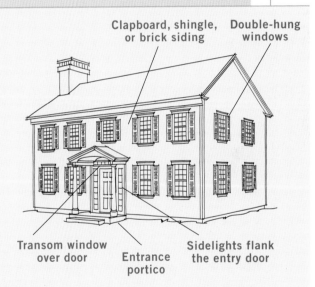

Clapboard, shingle, or brick siding

Double-hung windows

Transom window over door

Entrance portico

Sidelights flank the entry door

IN THE LATTER PART OF the 1800s, Americans witnessed a rebirth of historic architecture, much like what's happening today. Among the most popular revivals was the two-story Colonial. Colonial Revival houses are a retrospective blend of the earlier Georgian and Adam styles, and they share the originals' symmetry and the traditionally arranged formal and informal spaces. The newer style added an entry portico with classically influenced columns and a door with an elliptical transom overhead flanked by tall, narrow sidelight windows.

Some Colonial Revival homes have the hipped roof of the French Colonial style but with only a slight overhang. Many have the gable roof of the northern Colonials, often with a crossgable to place greater emphasis on the central portion of the house and the entry door. Although the Colonial Revival followed the basic hallmarks of the originals, Americans also favored details from the Queen Anne, Italianate, and Greek Revival, creating eclectic variations. Some houses were so significantly modified that you may not immediately recognize them as Colonial Revivals.

Because Colonial Revivals are a more recent style, reaching further into the nation's middle than earlier Colonials, many more of them remain in neighborhoods today. In fact, the time line between the Colonial Revival and the more recent postwar Colonial is blurred somewhat, as the style has virtually been in a nonstop state of progression since its introduction in 1880.

This new home was constructed with conventional lightweight framing, but the timber trusses high in the ceiling were added as a reference to past building methods and for the straightforward beauty of the massive joined timbers.

The Building Inspector

☆
PRACTICAL MATTERS

IF YOU'RE NOT FAMILIAR with the local building code (more of a building *law*, in fact), then you need to speak with the building inspector. This individual can steer you toward a copy of the building code handbook that's in effect for your particular town or city.

The building code is very complicated, regulating everything from the size of fireplace hearthstones to the size of bedroom windows. The companion National Electrical Code regulates such things as the number and spacing of electrical outlets along a new kitchen countertop, and the National Plumbing Code determines the amount of water used to flush a toilet. If you design a home or addition without the

help of professionals, it is absolutely essential to know every subtle nuance of the local building code. Mistakes have to be torn out and rebuilt, and, more important, you could be jeopardizing the safety of your family.

sometimes prohibit such decisions, because there may be a costly impact on the structure and nearby rooms. If modifications get very ambitious, the architect or contractor may simply suggest tearing down the structure and starting over.

If your budget allows, and your property is big enough, you can create a no-compromise fantasy home that will satisfy your every whim. The Colonial can live up to Dream Home potential without fuss or missing tempo. However, don't be tempted to trade quality for extra square footage. One of the biggest mistakes you can make is blowing the budget on sheer size, while leaving the important details and finishing touches to the imagination.

Building with integrity

Constructing a new home enables you to take advantage of the latest in building technologies, from maniacally efficient furnaces to slender wiring capable of linking the Internet, phone systems, security systems, and even the home's lighting controls to your home computer. Building codes have contributed substantially to energy conservation, resulting in houses that are better insulated, require less energy to heat and cool, and thus cost less to keep comfortable.

The design of casual family spaces that are often desired in new Colonials today needs to be tempered with places for quiet retreat. While a bedroom can provide sanctuary on an upper floor, a closeable study or home office can do the same on the floor below.

The continuous expanse of hardwood flooring, running throughout the rooms of this Colonial, emphasizes the open feeling of the plan, visually stretching the distance from one end of the home to the other.

true-divided-light — A traditional window sash with dividing muntin and individual panes of glass.

Conventions in wood framing have also improved, as architects and contractors create stronger buildings with 2x6 wood studs in wall construction, superseding common 2x4s. Conventional floor decks and roof systems are being replaced with strong, stable, manufactured joists, beams, and rafters. Manufactured structural products are wood and resin composites, efficiently produced from chipped or shredded new-growth, harvested trees, with virtually no waste. And they're less prone to shrinkage, eliminating many of a home's cracks and pops.

A vast number of window manufacturers compete for your attention by constantly upgrading their products.

The majority of windows and exterior doors available today are well-engineered, attractive products, produced in custom shapes and sizes in a range of options. Wood windows with **true-divided-lights** are well suited to traditional houses such as the Colonial. A low-maintenance alternative is an aluminum-clad wood window; clad windows come in many durable colors and are especially helpful in coastal environments, where they foil the effects of dampness and salty air.

Planning to meet your needs

Designing a new home with a past as time-honored as the Colonial doesn't mean you'll be forced into closed-up spaces or an inefficient floor plan. You can plan ahead for all of the activities you want to include in your life and let the floor plan take shape from there. Part of the Colonial's legacy is its adaptability over the centuries. The interior spaces can be as widely open to one another as you prefer. Or you can create discrete public rooms in the traditional way for formal entertaining, while opening the back, private area of the home to casual living, abundant natural light, and communication between spaces.

The size of your Colonial depends on both the need for space and the amount of money available to build your new home. Even if you can muster a generous budget, you may choose to keep the size modest. Many architects and homeowners have proven that by allowing activities to overlap, or by hosting a number of activities in the same space, it's possible to accomplish a lot on a relatively small footprint. You may have visited jumbo Colonials that have a separate room for every imaginable activity, creating a redundancy of playrooms, family rooms, bonus rooms, media rooms, sunrooms, recreation rooms, game rooms, billiard rooms, living

Natural wood siding, wood windows, and wood trim details contribute to a faithful appearance appropriate for all Colonial styles. Regional practices can help you decide how to narrow down your specific choices for a house that fits within the local context.

rooms, sitting rooms, parlors, conservatories, libraries, studies, and dens. For most of us, furnishing just half of these rooms would require the sale of several offspring.

And speaking of offspring, just how spread out through the home do you really want your children to be? I've found that the joys and best memories of family life have to do with *togetherness* rather than *apartness*. The home you design should promote interaction while allowing a room for escape or a quiet conversation

during hectic times—a dual function that comes naturally to the public/private personality of the Colonial.

Every Colonial has its place

Our choices for construction materials and products have become homogenized from coast to coast, meaning you can purchase the same lumber, masonry, siding, or roofing in Ashland, Oregon, as you can in Millbrook, New York. The boundaries of regional architectural styles have thinned to faint dashes, and any style of

☆ Building In Convenience

AS YOU SKETCH BIG IDEAS for your new home's major spaces, keep in mind the small touches that can make daily life more pleasant:

★ Half my clients place the laundry room upstairs, where all the towels, sheets, and clothes are. The other half prefer the laundry room near the kitchen, where the machines are within earshot and close by. With the advent of full-size, stackable machines you can have a compact laundry closet on both floors for ultimate convenience.

★ Include a mudroom with plenty of space, and include a comfortable bench for slipping in and out of shoes. You might add a broom closet, coat closet, sports closet,

and individual cubbies for the children's book bags (and one for a friend), boot storage, and an extra refrigerator.

★ Provide a shelf or countertop between the garage and kitchen where you can set down a couple of grocery bags.

★ Install a cold water tap on the wall behind your cooktop, making it unnecessary to carry a heavy pot from the sink to the stove every time you prepare pasta or boil lobster.

★ Construct thick walls between the major first-floor rooms to accommodate shelves. It's a great way to create storage, and the wall depth, noticeable in passageways, will give a substantial heft to your home.

★ Install a dedicated stair from the second floor to the attic, instead of the pull-down type, to make for an easier, safer trip to the top of the house.

★ Include deep windowsills in highly visible locations to display objects that look wonderful in the sunlight, such as potted plants or a favored decorative glass piece.

This guesthouse sits near its counterpart and mimics the traditional shape and a few historic details of Colonials in the region.

Colonial can be constructed nearly anywhere. But regional architectural character still exists, and regional methods are still in use. The practice of using metal roofs in Vermont, brick walls in North Carolina, and beaded clapboard siding in Newport, Rhode Island, contributes to the distinctive character of those parts of the nation. Your new Colonial has a lengthy heritage which can be expressed through the arrangement of the main house and appendages, through the shape of the roof, and by referencing traditional details—either literally or in the abstract. As you embark on the design decisions of your new home, consider the context, or,

region, in which you live, and the choices you face will become to a few obvious answers.

In recent years, homeowners have shown a surge of interest in homes with the pleasing proportions and interesting architectural features of earlier Colonial styles. The new homes in this chapter are examples of this rising awareness of our architectural heritage. Today's Colonial homes aren't slaves to the style, however. They are *inspired* by the trials and errors of multiple generations and use only the features that make sense for how we live today.

Summer
on Nantucket

ABOVE, **A brand-new home** on the peaceful island of Nantucket conjures up the memory of carefree summer afternoons with sand caught between your toes. A simple double-hung window frames a view across the treetops to the ocean beyond. The kneewall beneath the sloped ceiling makes use of the abundant storage concealed in the low eaves.

FACING PAGE, **The siting of the home** creates a rare intimacy near the sidewalk, far different from the typical suburban home, which is usually buffered from pedestrians and the street with an expansive lawn.

A N EXTRAORDINARY FAMILY GETAWAY lies on the tiny island of Nantucket, about 30 miles south of Cape Cod, Massachusetts. The island is host to an affable New England community drawn by picturesque surroundings and peaceful seaside living. This is where Peg and Philip live during the warm-weather months. Their stately, yet casual, Colonial merges seamlessly with the historic fabric of the island architecture. It's no surprise when the day-trippers who stroll the charming brick walks mistake their house for a restored classic. Careful attention to proportioning, the selective use of historic elements, and a sensitivity to the local **vernacular** have shaped this new home into what appears to be a time-honored "islander."

TRADITIONAL VALUE

The house is sited very close to the street, as are the other houses in the neighborhood, creating a comfortable corridor between the building facades and the street edge. Objects are scaled to pedestrians rather than

vernacular ⌐ The original architecture or design motifs that were developed in specific regions by the original inhabitants.

ABOVE, **The side walls** of New England homes were sometimes clad in relatively inexpensive shingles while the front facade was covered in wood clapboard for a formal presentation to the street. The hinged wood shutters add to the home's authentic historic appearance.

cars, such as low picket fences, potted flowers, mailboxes, and lamp posts. Even the brick sidewalks and driveways relate to a human being, with a quilt of individual pieces about the size of your hand instead of the usual strip of concrete or asphalt.

Peter Zimmerman and his staff of architects followed the practice of emphasizing the symmetrical Colonial facade by avoiding overlapping or competing building forms. To the rear of the house, however, the architects used an arrangement of rambling "additions" to mimic the character of an older home. The design suggests that previous generations outgrew the house and added a porch or an extension as the demand arose.

The new house is largely clad in white cedar shingles, a typical island siding material. In the sun-saturated, salty air, the shingles quickly weather to a pleasant silvery gray tone. The side facing the street is covered in painted cedar clapboards. The use of the more refined clapboard on only the front facade is a nod to a frugal, age-old Yankee custom.

A FULL HOUSE

This summer place sees a lot of activity. The owners are siblings of families with seven children each, and they are raising three boys of their own. Every weekend, a

new set of brothers and sisters, nephews and nieces, grandparents and in-laws arrive by ferry to spend time at the getaway. With a full house, the plan needed to allow young and old to socialize comfortably. The architect accomplished this by establishing two large living areas, one at the formal front of the house and a more relaxed family room to the rear, where there is good access to the backyard. The kitchen is central and easily accessed from either living space. During a busy evening, children and teenagers can spread out in the family room while parents socialize in the front room. The remaining formal room to the front of the house, across from the center hall, is a study where family members can escape the hubbub for an intimate con-

Interior woodwork does a lot to establish the tone within a house. Although the family room is a casual destination, the theme of painted woodwork is carried to this area for a sense of continuity throughout the home. Built-in cabinets to one side hold books, games, and the television, hidden neatly behind a paneled enclosure.

A painted wood mantle surrounds the fireplace in the customary Colonial manner and is complemented by the trim and ceiling beams. The living room's wide passageway offers good connectivity to the rest of the home.

versation or a private phone call. Philip keeps a home office in this quiet spot, so he can keep up with professional commitments while enjoying a full summer in paradise.

There are two staircases climbing to the bedrooms above, ensuring open lanes for the heavy traffic that occurs while hosting summer guests. Peg attributes the successful flow of the floor plan to the extra stair. The drawing below shows how the rear stair is positioned directly across from the back entry door, making for an easy escape to the village or the beach without having to traverse the entire house.

SIMPLE AND SERENE

Peg will tell you that a key to creating a vacation retreat is to *simplify*. She chose to avoid clutter and too many

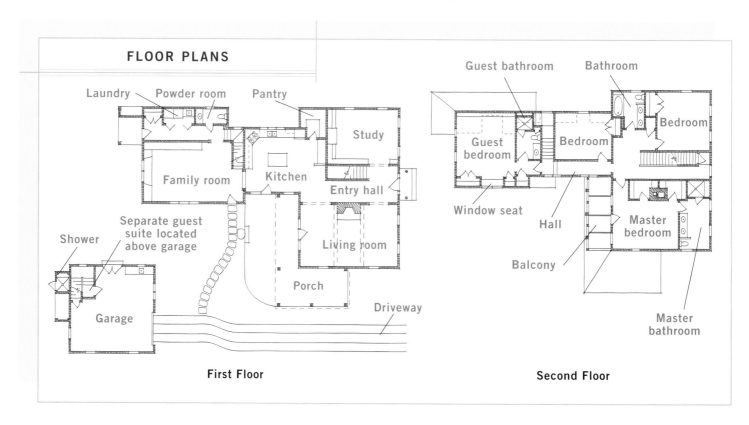

FLOOR PLANS

Laundry Powder room Pantry

Study

Family room Kitchen

Entry hall

Separate guest suite located above garage

Shower

Living room

Porch

Garage

Driveway

First Floor

Guest bathroom Bathroom

Guest bedroom

Bedroom

Bedroom

Window seat

Hall

Balcony

Master bedroom

Master bathroom

Second Floor

This classic central hall is nicely appointed but deliberately understated to reflect its casual summer-home setting. The entry welcomes you in and provides a sunny glimpse of the rooms beyond.

Kitchen Surfaces

NATURAL STONE COUNTERTOPS are enjoying an unprecedented popularity in kitchen design today. The hard, smooth materials are durable, wipe up easily, won't harbor bacteria, and can't be marred by hot cookware. Plus, they offer unique characteristics as well as beauty.

Slate, available in several colors, offers a satiny surface at a relatively reasonable price. It will develop a time-worn patina, absorbing cooking oils and showing some scratches.

Soapstone is soft and amazingly workable. And if your counters become scratched, you can fix them with fine sandpaper. Soapstone resists stains and is slightly more expensive than slate; it ranges narrowly in the gray palette, commonly with streaks of green, white, or black. A recommended coating of mineral oil turns the stone a deep charcoal black.

Marble has a great variety of natural colors and vein patterns to match almost any kitchen. It is less prone to staining than slate and will keep a polished appearance for a long time, but it is costly.

Granite is understated but comes in a wide range of colors and textures. It is highly resistant to staining, and is available polished or honed. Although expensive, it will last a lifetime.

accessories for a minimalist look—in a traditional manner of course. The first-floor rooms are serene spaces, decorated with comfortable chairs, built-in architectural details, and pale, sun-washed colors. Upstairs, the bedroom walls are painted in a classic bright white and subtle shades of blue. The color choices do much more than set the tone as a favorite seaside decorating scheme. The lightly painted walls reflect light, emphasizing the complexion of a sunny ocean environment. The trim, beaded **wainscot,** and the interior louvered shutters come to life in the play of light and shadow, revealing the beauty of the pattern and texture inherent in the architecture.

Peg and Philip hope that their getaway will provide refuge and rest for many generations to come. They've certainly set the stage, with a home that takes its place in a venerable community sensitive to its architectural heritage. No one will ever have to know that theirs is just a first-generation home, thanks to established Colonial planning principles and the architect's eye for accurate detailing and proportion.

wainscot ⁀ A decorative interior treatment, often of wood, that emphasizes and protects the lower portion of a wall.

Dutch Treat

ABOVE, **A convenient entry** from the garage leads up the stairs to the kitchen. The connection between the kitchen and where the cars are parked is an essential relationship in the design of any new home.

FACING PAGE, **A Dutch Colonial** in Newport, Rhode Island, expresses a traditional heritage and achieves a calm harmony with the landscape.

Yankee gutter — Two planks of wood assembled in a V shape and installed to the eaves of a roof to direct rainwater.

A QUIET COLONIAL HOME IN NEWPORT, Rhode Island, sits on a small knoll, peeking from behind the outreaching canopy of a 200-year-old copper beech tree. The house is entirely new—but you might not know it. The design is timeless, with such details as wood **Yankee gutters,** bold window casings, and a front facade clad in painted clapboard.

Peter and Dorrie built the home on part of an old estate, choosing a small parcel that had been the location of the cutting garden. It wasn't long before a bright and hardy Dutch Colonial sprang from the rich, fertile loam. They had performed minor renovations on a couple of earlier homes but had never built from scratch—or with such ambition. Long-time friend and builder Frank DiMauro suggested the couple become their own contractors, while his son Ron, an architect, would lead the development of the design. Frank himself took on the role of mentor and framer.

As with any successful collaboration, a thorough and common understanding of the project's goals is crucial. Ron and Frank began by asking the kinds of questions that would enable the couple to better visualize their new house. Peter and Dorrie knew they wanted a structure that would age gracefully and fit in well with

the Newport vernacular. In particular, they were committed to working carefully around the copper beech tree at the corner of the property. They desired a floor plan that would flow well for entertaining, and they wished to explore the elegant sensibility of **Shaker** design. Last, Dorrie handed Ron an illustration from the children's book *A Home,* by Carl Larsson, as inspiration for the design of the dining-room fireplace and the cozy den.

ESTABLISHING THE GROUND RULES

A building site's natural topography and vegetation are often considered a hindrance and a headache by developers and building contractors. That's why the landscape of many developments is stripped clean. It's more economical to build on a flattened landscape than to work around mounds, outcrops, and mature trees. After the bare site has been developed, shrubs and saplings can be dotted here and there with the hope of a "natural" look.

Peter and Dorrie directed that their site be respectfully developed, and the result is a home with a much more rooted appearance. The new design incorporates established garden beds from the old estate at either side of the front door, and a rock garden in view of the new screened porch at the back of the house.

THE PLANNING STRATEGY

Peter and Dorrie's new home is perfectly suited for two, as well as for entertaining large groups. At the modest size of about 1,450 sq. ft. on the first level, the floor plan functions like a much larger home. This is

Shaker — A quiet religious sect known for their remarkably simple yet beautiful furniture.

The link to the garage steps down with the slope of the site, which keeps this large structure in scale with the main house. Native plantings in terraced beds line the stone walkway to the front door.

A box bay provides plenty of light and offers a tempting spot for a quiet read. Beneath the seat is a storage area for blankets, while the depth of the bay visually extends the space.

accomplished by linking rooms with large passageways. If you look at the plan on p. 164, you'll notice a continuous circular path throughout the entire floor without dead ends. This enables guests to meander and mingle uninhibited from room to room, and for the hosts to slip back and forth conveniently from entertaining to the behind-the-scenes activity of the kitchen.

Ron introduced a touch of spatial variety in the entry hall, creating a high ceiling that is lit by one of the many small dormer windows along the front of the home (see the bottom photo on p. 166). A display niche surrounds the window and is centered over the entry door, and the alignment of these features lends the entry an air of formality.

The screened porch off the kitchen at the back of the house commands a view over the rock garden below.

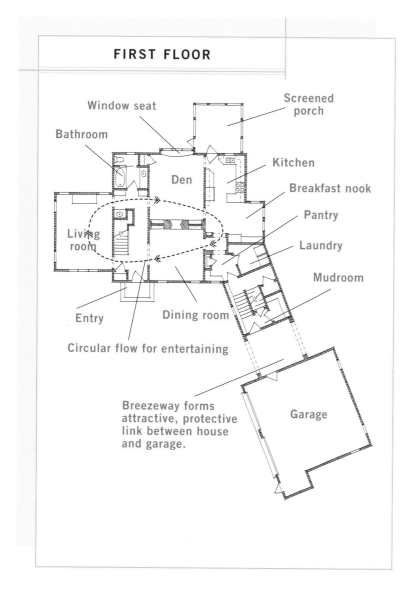

FIRST FLOOR

Window seat

Bathroom

Screened porch

Den

Kitchen

Breakfast nook

Pantry

Living room

Laundry

Mudroom

Entry

Dining room

Circular flow for entertaining

Breezeway forms attractive, protective link between house and garage.

Garage

The handcrafted stair reveals a few surprises. A panel at the landing hinges downward, unfolding steps to access the storage attic over the living room. Beneath the stair, a trapezoidal paneled door opens to a space for storing odds and ends.

Across from the door is a staircase that leads up and over an arched opening. The arch is a passageway that leads to the back of the house and frames a built-in bookcase that Peter handcrafted in his basement workshop.

The bookcase isn't Peter's only home project. While traveling in South America, Peter and Dorrie had been charmed by a small armoire displayed in a Brazilian museum. Peter sketched the piece and later recreated it in Brazilian Parana pine. It's one of several projects Peter has built for the home. Another piece, inspired by South American refectory tables, sits in the dining room. Peter incorporated scrolled metal kneebraces, found in a Brazilian flea market, into the design.

The built-in projects throughout the home exhibit a simplicity much like the Shaker aesthetic the couple enjoys so much. The door and window casings, among

ABOVE, **A small space for sharing** a meal and perhaps a section or two of the Sunday paper is combined with a kitchen desk where grocery lists can be prepared, bills paid, and house keys dropped off.

LEFT, **The barnlike garage** is connected to the main house with a breezeway. The graceful arch of the opening frames the view of a copper beech tree—which, according to the architect, has occupied the site for over 200 years.

Cupolas

CUPOLAS ARE THE BANTAM roof structures that adorn the tops of many Colonial homes, garages, and barns across the country. While they serve as a highly decorative cap to a plain roofline, cupolas also had the practical value of venting hot air from a stuffy attic. A larger cupola with windows on all sides can be used to introduce natural light dramatically into a room. This is a richer daylighting solution than a common skylight and can be styled in a variety of ways for a timeless, traditional appearance or for a fresh, contemporary look.

other trim details, share this absence of superfluous detail. The resulting continuity of expression is evident throughout.

A LIGHT FROM ABOVE

The house is topped by a 6-ft.-high cupola. At night, the light from the cupola can be seen from the nearby coastline. "It's a beacon for the home," Ron says. He designed the structure, with its bell-shaped roof, then crafted it along with his father and Peter during the evening hours. Peter fondly remembers the time spent creating this crowning element, and the cupola stands as a symbol for the collaboration between homeowner and architect, father and son.

The entry hall greets visitors with a spatial surprise—the ceiling rises beyond the second-floor line, revealing the dormer window above. The light draws the eye upward, where the niche surrounding the window creates a shelf for display.

The dining room is located to the front of the home in the traditional manner. This formal room was kept small in size to allow more space for the everyday rooms. The sideboard and the cabinet visible through the opening were built by the owner in his home workshop.

Freedom of Expression

ABOVE, **This master bedroom** is within the second story of this tower. Windows positioned over the balcony door admit light from high above, as in other rooms of the home. From this vantage point, the owner can survey the garden rooms below and the distant views beyond.

FACING PAGE, **An explosion of light** and color is bottled within the interior of this Colonial inspired home. This is the great room, where dining and living are combined in one.

R EMEMBER THE MOMENT IN *The Wizard of Oz* when the screen turns from black and white to brilliant color? As you enter the home of John and his best friend, Buster, in rural northeastern Connecticut, you're apt to have something of that exhilarating feeling. John worked with architect Alexander Gorlin to create what was to be a rustic weekend retreat, but the getaway is now his permanent address—and his dream home.

WE'RE NOT IN KANSAS ANYMORE

John and Buster's Colonial-influenced house is a sprawling assembly of vernacular forms adding up to about 3,500 sq. ft. of living space. From a distance, the villagelike enclave looks as though it had been seated here comfortably for the last two centuries. But this is a new home, spread along its site to visually cut down the potential mass of the structure. The individual "houses" touch one another at corners or along the lower floor walls. To one side, a garage with a guest house is connected to the entry by only a garden pergola, lining up along the driveway in the way that a colonnade flanks a village square. John's color scheme

The understated exterior, with its gray tones of weathered shingles, clapboard, and plastered chimneys, cloaks the lively environment within.

for the fragmented structure is a monochromatic blending of gray tones, with a rugged, weathered appearance something like stone. The window sashes are painted a dark hunter green to merge with the deep hues of the tree canopies reflected in the glass.

The house's entry sets the scene for the dramatic use of space. You pass beneath a low shed roof into a spacious hall with a fireplace. John studied the Early American homes of Williamsburg, Virginia, and was influenced by the function of the Southern entry halls of long ago. These were spaces where the family business was conducted and often contained a desk and chairs. John uses his entry hall in a similar way—it performs double-duty, serving also as a comfortable home office.

A sudden burst of real-life Technicolor® awaits those who venture farther into the home. The great room

ceiling soars nearly 25 ft., supported by a series of heavy wood trusses that also carry lighting for the large space. Sunlight is admitted through groups of clerestory windows high above the floor. The room is subtly divided into dining and living areas by a long, low built-in cabinet that contains John's sizable collection of art, books, and antiques.

At the far wall of the great room, an unobstructed panel of glass sits atop the fireplace where there ought to be a chimney. The window frames a distant view and is cleverly positioned in the way a portrait might be placed above the mantle. John created long vistas from each of the major rooms in his home by selective cutting and pruning the trees on the property. "Each view is unique," John explains. "From the great room, you can see the Housatonic River. From my bedroom, the clerestory windows frame the stars." In fact, each

RIGHT, **Places for art** and comfortable seating are tucked in throughout the home. In the master bedroom, the owner's pal Buster poses before an alcove created by the placement of two closets.

BELOW, **The kitchen is dramatized** with accent lighting along fiery walls and gleaming stainless steel. Though the home appears to be two stories throughout, it's constructed largely on one level, providing plenty of opportunity for tall spaces and cathedral ceilings.

Each of the rooms uses windows placed high in the walls to allow natural light to flood in from above.

window is a portrait of an ever-changing landscape, interspersed with the owner's collection of painted pieces hung on the walls.

THERE'S NO PLACE LIKE HOME

The kitchen is positioned behind the dining room and is large enough to hold a large group when John entertains. Entertaining is often casual in this home. For example, the low cabinet dividing the great room serves as a buffet during a party. Extending from the kitchen is a screened porch, which is large enough to hold a table and a small seating group. The porch catches the sunset and has become a favorite spot for a late-evening meal during the summer. John notes, "Every view has its best hour."

This rambling home can accommodate several overnight guests if necessary. There is a complete suite

The entry offers glimpses of the light-filled rooms beyond. Trimwork is used sparingly, limited to door and window casings, except in the great room, where John added a thin band of picture molding at the level of the upper windowsills.

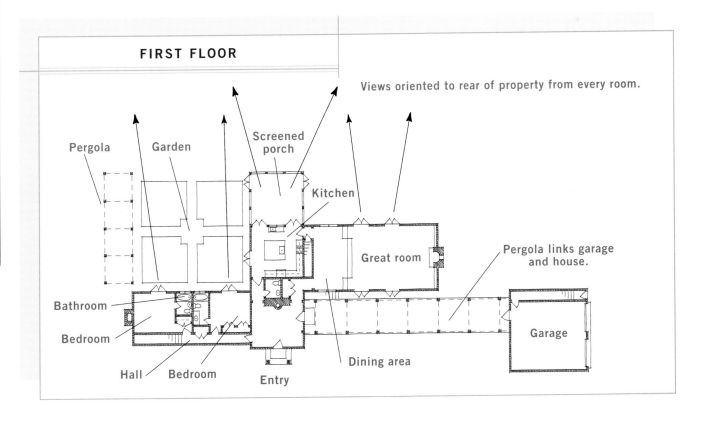

FIRST FLOOR

Views oriented to rear of property from every room.

Pergola

Garden

Screened porch

Kitchen

Great room

Pergola links garage and house.

Bathroom

Bedroom

Garage

Hall   Bedroom   Entry

Dining area

A screened porch projects from the rear of the kitchen. The temple-like structure sets off spaces for garden rooms to either side, allowing a variety of views.

over the garage, and two bedrooms with their own baths in a wing extending from the entry hall. The master bedroom occupies a second-floor tower positioned over the wing. The tower shape contributes to the village atmosphere of the enclave and gives John a good view of the gardens close by and the river in the distance.

John and Buster left the historic, architecturally rich, Beacon Hill section of Boston to live here full time, and John has enjoyed the chance to experiment with the architectural challenge of creating a new old Colonial, which has the look of a New England village compound.

LEFT AND FACING PAGE, **In a witty use of solid masonry** and invisible glass, a window creates an ever-changing portrait over the mantle. In winter, snowflakes seemingly fall into the fire. This chimney fools the eye, serving primarily as a vertical compositional element on the exterior. The gas fireplace exhausts through the small vent visible below.

Maryland Masterpiece

ABOVE, **The back of the house** gives way to sheets of glass, dramatically opening the interior to views of the Chesapeake Bay. Traditional dormers are arranged in a way that turns them into symbolic artifacts. The dormers, with a small square window in each, act as skylights, directing light down into the great room below.

FACING PAGE, **The glazed rear wall** of the great room wraps the corner without the aid of a structural column, emphasizing the floating effect of the canopy-like ceiling.

T HOUGH A MODERNIST AT HEART, architect Hugh Newell Jacobsen, an internationally recognized master of the art and profession, explains that he likes his buildings to fit in. When he designed this Maryland home, he had already investigated the region's farmhouses and other indigenous buildings as precedents for the new design. He had also walked the site with his clients, Thomas and Robin, in tow. He recalls the winter day when they made the visit: "The ground was hard as concrete, it was cold as hell, but I immediately found the axis of the site. It brought me down to the water's edge, and I knew at that moment what the design of this building would be. The site told me everything I needed to know about the house's organization." The body of water Hugh came upon was the spectacular Chesapeake Bay, along with a view up the picturesque Hunting River.

A CLUSTER OF PAVILIONS

At first glance, Thomas and Robin's Maryland home resembles the rambling farmsteads of the surrounding area. There is a main house with a steeply pitched roof and a tall chimney rising from one side, with similar but

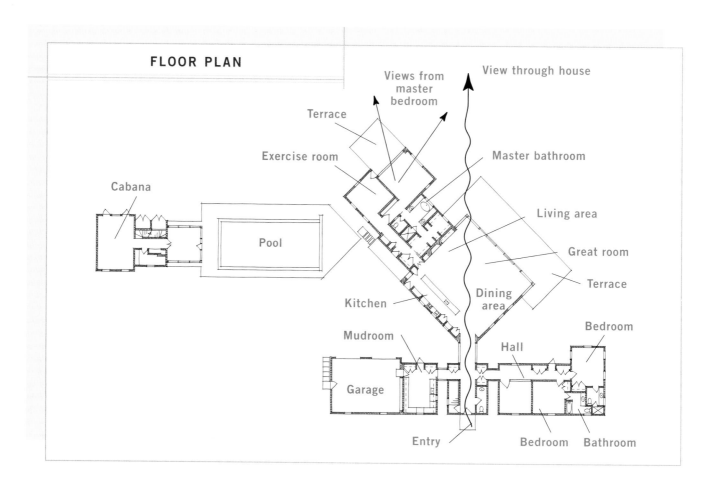

FLOOR PLAN

Cabana

Pool

Terrace

Exercise room

Views from master bedroom

View through house

Master bathroom

Living area

Great room

Terrace

Kitchen

Dining area

Mudroom

Hall

Bedroom

Garage

Entry

Bedroom

Bathroom

smaller structures grouped around. All are clad in time-honored materials, such as painted wood clapboard and wood trim. The true-divided-light windows are small and stingy, like those in colonists' early homes, and appear as punched openings in the plain facades. Although this home has been inspired by dwellings of old, a closer look reveals that the traditional architecture of the region has been daringly reinterpreted and woven into an engaging mesh of native familiarity and symbolic abstraction. The result is an entirely modern plan, combined with such unusual exterior features as the starkly geometric chimney, dormers arranged on the roof in an unusual formation, and, at the back of the largest structure, a wall that isn't quite there—just

panels of glass running around corners and from floor to eaves.

The various functions of the home are carried out in several distinct pavilions, strung like pearls along invisible passageways. The technique reduces the apparent size of what otherwise might have been an imposing home and better integrates the house with the landscape. Hugh believes that when a new house is completed, the site should look better than it had before, a feat easier voiced than accomplished.

The architect meticulously unfolds the experience of arriving at this home by slyly masking the open plan and the water views from the driveway approach. The front facade is an austere barrier, fortified by a dense

RIGHT, **In the flanking pavilions,** the architect draws upon a form that resembles a child's drawing of a house. And the exterior materials used throughout are completely ordinary: clapboard siding, wood windows, and an asphalt roof. Elegance is achieved by the simplicity of the design rather than by ornamentation.

BELOW, **As picturesque as** a back-road country farm, this Maryland enclave blends symbolic Colonial imagery and traditional materials with a comfortable interior designed for the reality of a modern lifestyle.

allée of pear trees arranged parallel to the entry and the flanking pavilions. Only on traveling through the front door to stand within the two-story hall are you awed with the view that inspired the architect and owners on that winter day. The vista continues through the passageway to an oversize great room and projects, uninterrupted, to the body of water beyond.

After taking in the remarkable view, the eye is lured upward. Two rows of miniature dormers are stacked like sentinels atop the roof, perforating the ceiling of the soaring space. They admit daylight far more artfully than any cluster of ordinary skylights.

Back at ground level, the fireplace wall includes paneled doors that open to reveal storage closets. The surrounding wall is covered with a painted wood grid, and on one side of the fireplace a grid-covered door cleverly opens to reveal a concealed passageway to another pavilion—Thomas and Robin's master bedroom suite.

ABOVE, **The towering entry** aligns visitors along the central axis of the home, directing them to the comfortable great room and the grand view beyond. To each side are narrower passages that lead to the private areas of the home—the guest bedroom wing to the right and the utility areas to the left.

RIGHT, **The private nature** of the site affords the owners the opportunity of a view uninterrupted by fabrics or blinds. The room is angled to emphasize the panoramic view, while the panels of floor-to-ceiling glass thrust the owners into the natural setting.

As in many of Jacobsen's houses, the great room becomes a theatrical backdrop to which the owner can carry out the drama of real life. The white interior scheme is expected to be enlivened by the books, decorative objects, and art that the owners will bring to the space.

This bedroom, like the great room, offers views down the bay and up the river; and again, the room's solid walls give way to full-height panels of glass, blurring the line between inside and out.

This project is an improbable marriage between Modernism and traditional architecture. It's a more dynamic mix than most—between the "groom," a handsome gable-roofed enclave, and the "bride," lovely and liberated, open and sharing. For Thomas and Robin, the merging of such uncertain personalities is a miracle coupling.

In the Spirit of the Style

The dormers in the upstairs rooms form deep wells for snug, comfortable window seats. The depth was created by building a second interior wall parallel to the exterior wall of the home.

C AN YOU CAPTURE THE SPIRIT of a Colonial house without building in the universal pattern of the Colonial style? Can you redesign the floor plan and still make it fit within the basic Colonial form? Can you rearrange the facade, rethink the **fenestration,** and reinvent the entry while hanging on to the familiar impressions that help us identify a Colonial? Architect Robert Reed used his creative problem-solving skills to resolve a difference in style preferences between him and his wife, Rhonda—and they came up with a brand new home that answers yes to all of these.

RETHINKING HOW A HOUSE WORKS

When the couple found a picturesque wooded site 30 miles outside of Seattle, each had ideas already in place. Rhonda favored a traditional image of home, while Robert was drawn to the crisp details and geometries of contemporary architecture. Luckily, there were major areas of agreement. Because their budget for construction was limited, they knew the new house would have to be relatively compact, with a floor plan that emphasized versatility. There could be no extrane-

fenestration ⌐ The placement and details of a structure's windows.

Architect Robert Reed combined storybook charm with crisp geometries in a compact new house that follows the basic model of a two-story Colonial dwelling.

The home's diminuitive footprint goes unnoticed in this spacious sequence of interior rooms. Functions stay defined within the open-plan arrangement, yet the shared space visually enlarges the entire house.

ous rooms that sat unused. Limiting floor area would mean rooms would have to be open to one another to create a sense of spaciousness. And because little ones were in the picture, the couple wanted every opportunity to provide inspiring spaces to enrich their children's imaginations.

While Robert sees this Colonial-inspired home as contemporary, Rhonda finds traditional charm in the steeply pitched roof and the prominent dormers. The roof pitch is a soaring 14 in 12, which tells us the angle exceeds 45 degrees. It also means there are a lot of possibilities in how the ceilings of the upper floor can be shaped. Because the house is small, and every square inch must be used, Robert incorporated a variety of ceiling heights for interest. There are cathedral ceilings in most of the rooms upstairs to avoid a cramped feeling and to create an enchanted storybook atmosphere for their three children. On the first floor he plays a trick by raising the kitchen floor 6 in., effectively diminishing the ceiling height. The effect also changes the perspective of the cook, allowing a view down to the table area via a wide pass-through to the dining area.

Robert's design assigns a large main space for an entry and dining. Adjacent to the front door is an inglenook, a charming traditional feature the couple had always promised to themselves. This is a great place to chat with a close friend or to sit and read by a crackling fire. The family room is around the corner from the fireplace. It satisfies the need for both entertaining space and a spot for relaxation—the budget didn't allow for a separate living room. That suits Robert and

Compact rooms don't mean dull spaces—the playful design of this children's bed invigorates the imagination for young family members.

While working in this kitchen, the cook enjoys a commanding perspective of guests and family. Although the kitchen occupies an interior area within the home, it escapes a closed-in feeling with views to other rooms and through nearby windows along the front facade.

Rhonda just fine, because they live a casual lifestyle. To avoid a constant mountain of children's toys from migrating into the space, an open playroom was included in the design of the second floor. Instead of the usual room titles of living room and family room, these spaces could be called "adults' room" and "children's room."

The couple chose to construct their home on a concrete slab, avoiding the cost of excavating a full basement. Without a below ground area in which to stash things, they came up with several unusual storage solutions. A compact hot-air furnace is located in a small closet under the stair, hidden behind a series of removable panels that, when closed, form a decorative pattern—there's no hint of a door. Robert also placed an outdoor storage closet in a porch column (see the plan on p. 188), a handy space for storing potting supplies

ABOVE, **Every inch of available** space is used in this efficiently crafted home. The kitchen is well fitted with plenty of cabinets, the depth of the windowsill creates a handy shelf, and a tambour door opens to reveal additional storage within an interior wall.

LEFT, **A cozy nook** located adjacent to the kitchen holds a settee and table for everyday meals. Large windows directed to the play area outside enable the parents to prepare a sandwich while monitoring the children.

The stair is positioned across from the entry and offers a finely crafted visual treat. Though the interior is planned with modern concepts, the detailing includes traditional gestures expressed with familiar materials and forms.

and a few yard toys. In the kitchen wall, a tambour door opens to reveal storage for a countertop appliance. And in the bedrooms, window seats double as chests.

EXTERIOR MOTIVES

In the earlier project on pp. 120–127, the architect created porches and sheltering overhangs in the additive method. This Colonial uses a *subtractive* technique to carve out sheltering spaces from the main form. The front stoop is protected from the elements by a recessed area about 3 ft. deep. And a modest porch is nestled beneath the second floor just outside the dining room.

The facades are pleasing compositions that stray from the usual symmetrical Colonial pattern. Robert used horizontal bands at different levels to emphasize the base, middle, and top—attributes of Classical design. The bands, referred to as belt lines or belt courses, align the sills of the windows (and can be positioned at the

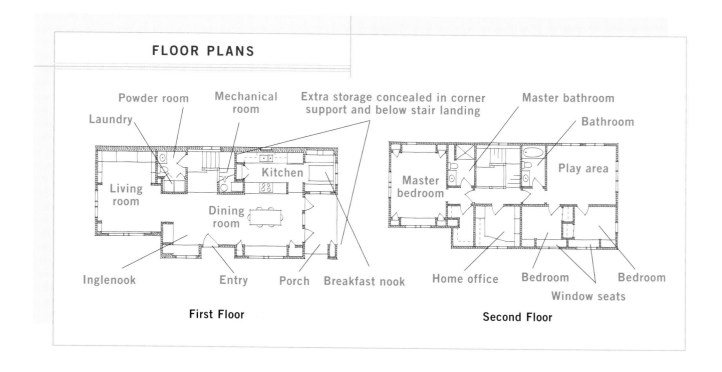

FLOOR PLANS

Powder room
Mechanical room
Extra storage concealed in corner support and below stair landing
Master bathroom
Bathroom
Laundry
Kitchen
Play area
Living room
Master bedroom
Dining room
Inglenook
Entry
Porch
Breakfast nook
Home office
Bedroom
Bedroom
Window seats

First Floor

Second Floor

A protected entry was created by recessing the door within the structure of the home rather than by adding a conventional portico. The covered area is just the right size for a small group of arriving guests and can accommodate a decorative display of potted plants. The glass door offers a welcome glow and a suggestion of the comfortable atmosphere within.

window heads), creating an orderly appearance. Below the first belt course, the material changes from shingle to smooth painted panels, which the architect uses to symbolize stone.

The windows are free of muntins to make the most of the view, and they work well with Robert's contemporary aesthetic. He used aluminum-frame windows because of a strict construction budget, but they are recessed into the wall to create depth and a richer

appearance. The simple, attractive mullion pattern in each of the windows adds interest by creating a recurring theme, and the extra transom above each provides additional light. This new house was the happy outcome to a common scenario. The husband and wife have disparate dream houses in mind, but only a single home can be constructed. The architect was able to bring about a successful compromise, merging charming imagery with clean and simple sensibilities.

CHAPTER FIVE

A FRESH PERSPECTIVE

ABOVE, **The vertical lines of the palms** act as a foil to the horizontal nature of the guest house.

FACING PAGE, **This Florida house** reveals its lineage with tall, slender windows, a hipped roof, extended over-hangs, and porches for shade, hinting back to the stick-built huts of French colonies in the West Indies.

T HE EVOLUTION OF THE COLONIAL HOUSE TYPE will continue, hand in hand with the ambitious march of technology, for generations to come. The possibilities haven't exhausted themselves just yet. Architects and homeowners are in an unremitting state of experimentation and discovery, which will keep shifting how we shape our homes—and our lifestyles. But as we move forward, we also cling to the familiar. It's part of our nature as human beings.

In recent years, traditional architecture has been liberated by removing walls and allowing spaces to stretch freely. Although few homeowners were eager to accept the tenets of modern design, they now universally seek open planning both for new houses and older Colonials built with tired concepts.

DECLARING INDEPENDENCE

A dramatic example of our changed thinking is this new house designed by Hugh Newell Jacobsen. The home sits quietly in the land of sunshine, just a chip

Postwar Colonial Hallmarks

AS UBIQUITOUS AS THE CAPE COD houses of Levittown, the postwar Colonial has been filling middle-class subdivisions and suburban lots since the end of World War II. It has long been a favored choice of builders (hence another name, the Builder's Colonial) as an easy-to-sell turn-key house. Like the Cape, it is also a relatively easy home to construct. The simple rectangular plan and the uniform facade make framing and specifying windows a snap. Construction of the two-story structure is relatively simple and fast, thanks to modern platform framing and premanufactured truss systems for the roof.

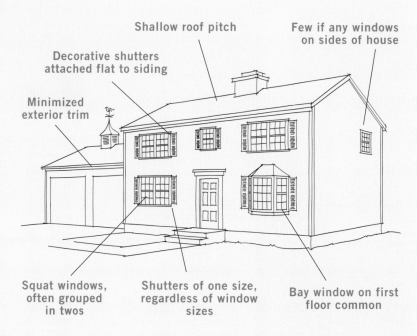

Shallow roof pitch

Few if any windows on sides of house

Decorative shutters attached flat to siding

Minimized exterior trim

Squat windows, often grouped in twos

Shutters of one size, regardless of window sizes

Bay window on first floor common

The builder's version is a different animal than the rest of the Colonial breed. Why? It typically lacks any hint of historic inspiration, and is disconnected, architecturally speaking. As the postwar building boom (and baby boom) emerged, developers and contractors realized that building fast and cheap filled a financially rewarding niche. Most homebuyers were young families just starting out, typically with little savings, and they were thrilled to have a place they could call their own.

The postwar Colonial was shaped by the constraints of cutting costs and construction time as well as by striving for maximum marketability. There seldom is much concern about siting to take advantage of land features, sunlight, and views. And details that might evoke a rich architectural heritage or even summon a simple charm are omitted for the sake of economy. These homes tend to be experienced as a *product* instead of a *place.* Still, with time and care, even a production-line Colonial can be turned into something special.

and a putt away from the Atlantic Ocean near Vero Beach, Florida. Quiet is the way Hugh prefers his buildings. He explains, "A building shouldn't shout to its neighbors." Hugh met his goal—the home he designed doesn't shout, but it *is* singing.

The form and imagery of this modern villa manage to fit within the distinctive Colonial genre—specifically, French Colonial, with a hip roof; wide overhangs for shade; tall, narrow windows; and high ceilings (the house has 10-ft. ceilings throughout). Even the symmetrical spacing of the windows fits neatly within the Colonial archetype. But as with his Maryland design on pp. 176–181, Hugh liberates the interior of the house with modern planning principles and excludes all applied ornamentation, such as decorative trim at the doors, windows, and ceiling line.

The house is energized by its blending of styles. For example, the symmetry of the front facade hearkens back to Colonials, and yet this isn't *really* the front—there is no entry door. The architect arranged this highly visible side of the house as a symbolic gesture, suggesting a connection with the past. It's a welcome reference because of its

ABOVE, **In a courtyard home,** the gate to the property becomes the front door. To complement this approach, the architect used tall wood doors with recessed panels that match the lanky proportions of window and door openings in the house.

LEFT, **The compact property** is completely filled by the courtyard and the new pavilion-like home. The courtyard wall connects two structures, one for the owners and one for guests, and makes the most of the outdoor space by creating an attractive enclosure for privacy.

LEFT, **The architect of this home** blended traditional, regional references with an expansive plan and a modern aesthetic. The swimming pool, located just a few inches from the living spaces, becomes part of the house and is a dramatic focal point both inside and out.

FACING PAGE, **The kitchen work areas** have views to the courtyard and pool, while cabinets and storage occupy the solid wall that faces nearby neighbors.

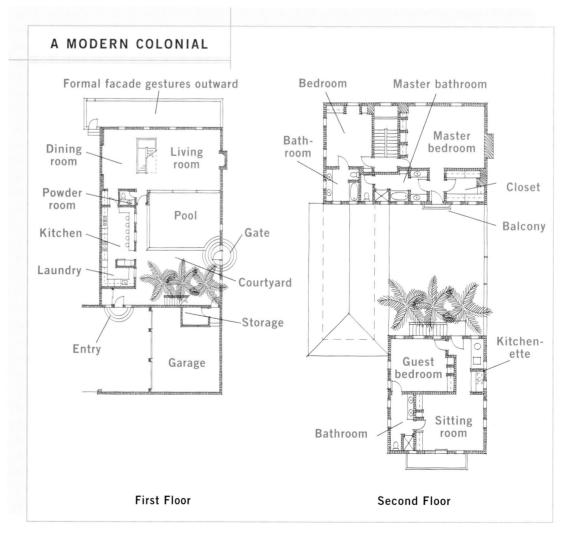

A MODERN COLONIAL

Formal facade gestures outward

Dining room
Living room
Powder room
Pool
Kitchen
Gate
Laundry
Courtyard
Storage
Entry
Garage

First Floor

Bedroom
Master bathroom
Bath-room
Master bedroom
Closet
Balcony
Kitchen-ette
Guest bedroom
Bathroom
Sitting room

Second Floor

familiarity. But once we step onto the compact site, we experience another vision altogether.

THIS IS NOT YOUR FATHER'S COLONIAL

The house is surrounded by garden walls, which enclose an interior courtyard and swimming pool. Two structures rise above the wall at opposite ends of the court: the main house and a detached guest house with a garage on the first floor. The pool and a palm garden link the structures and create one of the grandest

"rooms" on the property. Inside, there is an open plan for the living and dining area, separated by a sculptural stair that gives definition to the spaces while linking them visually. These rooms overlook the pool, which calmly laps at the base of a long glass-paneled wall. A wing extends from the structure along one edge of the courtyard to contain the kitchen and a laundry room. Windows in the kitchen are directed toward the private exterior space, while the opposite wall, facing the neighbor's property, is used for cabinets and other storage.

ABOVE, **A conventional stair** in this space would appear bulky and solid. This staircase achieves a weightless, transparent feeling by using open risers and a nearly invisible glass rail.

ABOVE, **The crisp lines** of the house are mirrored in the furniture selection for the bedroom, where the bed appears as a thin, wire-form cube—nearly a room within a room.

A VISIONARY HOME

The white monochrome interior reflects the Florida sun to such a degree that the home seems to emit its own light. The rail for the staircase is glass, adding to the drama of the seemingly endless transparency throughout the interior. The vast glazed area of the main space reflects the sparkle of the pool water and the dappled shade of the tall palms just outside. The floor-to-ceiling glass wall is set into a groove in the white concrete floor, allowing the floor to continue visually uninterrupted to the water's edge. The immediacy of the courtyard and pool achieves the often-sought goal of bringing the outside in—despite the marked contrast of the solid walled enclosure that surrounds the building.

The grid overlaying the facade aligns perfectly with the awning windows on the upper floor, the sash rails of the lower floor windows, and the shallow brackets extending beneath the soffit—an indication of the architect's skill.

A PRIVATE SUITE FOR GUESTS

The guest house contains a bedroom, bathroom, kitchenette, and a gracious sitting room with a balcony overlooking a nearby recreation field. The sitting room serves as an extra bedroom should the need arise. The entire suite is accessed by an outdoor staircase leading up from the courtyard behind the shelter of the palms.

Although the guest house appears to be clad in clapboard, the material is Hardie Board™, which Hugh describes as a wood substitute cast in cement. Wood is highly susceptible to mildew in the humid Florida climate, and this durable product is inexpensive and doesn't require the upkeep necessary for wood siding. The main house is clad in 4-ft. by 8-ft. Hardie Board panels for the same reason. A trellis in a geometric grid covers the vertical seams, helping keep the panel system weathertight.

Hugh often designs his homes in pavilion-like complexes. This one follows true to that philosophy,

even though the small site allowed for only two structures. Separating the required functions of the house
into smaller structures "eliminates the probability of
creating one big mother of a house," says Hugh. And,
interestingly, he finds it easier to accommodate a client's
request to change room sizes during the design phase
if the house is organized in this way; with a more
conventional home design, the whole concept might
be lost.

A NEW SENSIBILITY

Is this home a glimpse of how our children and grand-
children may be living in upcoming decades? Will we
visit them in modern pavilions with flowing, open floor
plans and walls of glass peering into private yards, while
familiar whispers of our architectural legacy linger quietly outside? The approach taken here, as with many of
the homes in the previous chapters, may be a foretaste
of a successful blending of familiar references with contemporary planning. Or perhaps it's a validation of what
has already arrived. The Colonial, in its many styles and
forms, has proven to be one of the most resilient house
types in architectural history and promises to accommodate nearly all we ask of it.

The Colonial has always presented a stoic image of
formality to the public side—and even this Vero Beach
house places its living and dining spaces behind an
orderly, symmetrical facade. The style shakes off this
dignified image toward the back of the house, where
additions reside informally in any number of shapes and
sizes. There is a dichotomy inherent in the style that is
undeniably apparent in human beings as well, suggesting there's more to the popularity of Colonial houses
than we may realize.

ABOVE, **The garden wall screens** the pool from
a nearby neighbor but offers a peek-through of
the street beyond through the narrow slit at left
and the square window in the center.

FACING PAGE, **The landscaping is integrated**
with the house, forming a triptych of regional
greenery before a spare canvas. The tall palms
afford privacy for the guest suite across the
courtyard.

Sources

FEATURED ARCHITECTS

Ace Architects
330 Second St., No. 1
Oakland, CA 94607
510-452-0775

David Barbour, Architect
109 Wall St.
Bridgeport, CT 06604
203-335-4474
pp. 41, 70–77

Centerbrook Architects and Planners
P.O. Box 955
Centerbrook, CT 06409
860-767-0175
pp. 11, 44 (bottom)

Ronald F. Dimauro, Architects, Inc.
28 Bellevue Ave.
Newport, RI 02840
401-846-6868
pp. 15, 149, 150, 160–169

F. Bradford Drake, AIA, Principal
RTKL Associates
1250 Connecticut Ave.
Washington, DC 20036
202-833-4400
pp. 6, 13

Alexander Gorlin, Architect
137 Varick St.
New York, NY 10003
212-229-1199
pp. 146, 168–175

Allan Greenberg, Architect, LLC
1600 K St. NW, Suite 500
Washington, DC 20006
202-785-4591
pp. 5, 9 (bottom), 39 (top)

Richard F. Hein, Architects and Associates
138 Larchmont Ave.
Suite 4, Floor 2
Larchmont, NY 10538
914-834-1414
pp. 12, 85, 135

Hugh Newell Jacobsen, Architect,
FAIA, PLLC
2529 P St., NW
Washington, DC 20007
202-337-5200
pp. 34, 38, 142, 143, 145, 151, 176–181,
190–199

Knight Associates Architects
157 Hinkley Ridge Rd.
Blue Hill, ME 04614
207-374-2845
pp. 25, 27, 87, 144

Robert B. Reed, Architect
4309 Olympic Blvd.
Everett, WA 98203
425-454-0566
pp. 36, 148, 182–189

Schoenhardt, Architects, Inc.
One Massaco Pl.
Simsbury, CT 06070
860-658-4496
p. 126

Anthony Terry, Architect
117 Northford Rd.
Branford, CT 06405
203-481-6424
Acknowledgements, pp. 1 (bottom), 120–127,
146 (bottom)

Z:Architecture
1052 Main St. Suite #12
Branford, CT 06405
203-488-8484
pp. 2, 9 (top), 12, 17, 26, 28–31, 35, 40, 42, 44
(top), 45–69, 78–83, 85–89, 90 (top), 93,
94–109, 134–141

Peter Zimmerman Architects
828 Old Lancaster Rd.
Berwyn, PA 19312
610-647-6970
pp. 1 (top), 3, 33, 39 (bottom), 128–133, 147,
152–159

DEVELOPER

HP Broom Housewright, Inc.
P.O. Box 70
Hadlyme, C T 06439
860-526-9836
pp. 10, 19–24, 84, cover

RELATED ORGANIZATIONS

The American Architectural Foundation
202-626-7318
www.archfoundation.org

The Colonial Williamsburg Foundation
757-229-1000
www.colonialwilliamsburg.org

The National Building Museum
202-272-2448
www.nbm.org

The National Trust for Historic Preservation
202-588-6000
www.nationaltrust.org

Preservation Society of Newport County
401-847-1000

Society for the Preservation of New England
Antiquities
617-227-3956
www.spnea.org

FURTHER READING

Allen, Edward, Joseph Aano. *Fundamentals of
Building Construction: Materials and Methods.*
New York: Wiley, 1998.

Chitham, Robert. *The Classical Orders of
Architecture.* New York: Rizzoli, 1985.

Cummings, Abbott Lowell. *The Framed
Houses of Massachusetts Bay, 1625-1725.*
Cambridge, Mass.: Belknapp Press of Harvard
University Press, 1979.

Kelly, J. Frederick. *Early Domestic Architecture of
Connecticut.* New York: Dover, 1963.

McAlester, Virginia and Lee. *A Field Guide to
American Houses.* New York: Knopf, 1996.

Morrison, Hugh. *Early American Architecture:
From the First Colonial Settlements to the
National Period.* New York: Oxford University
Press, 1952.

Norberg-Schulz, Christian. *The Concept of
Dwelling: On the Way to a Figurative
Architecture.* New York: Rizzoli, 1985.

Nylander, Jane C., Wendell Garrett, Davi
Bohl, and Diane Viera. *Windows on the Past:
Four Centuries of New England Homes.* Boston:
Bulfinch Press, 2000.

Roth, Leland M. *A Concise History of
American Architecture.* New York: Harper and
Row, 1979.

Susanka, Sarah. *Creating the Not So Big House.*
Newtown, CT: The Taunton Press, 2000.

Index

Note: Page numbers of references to material in photos/figures are shown in *italics*. Page ranges in *italics* (e.g. *180–81*) include references to both photos/figures and text.